BY THE WORD
OF THEIR TESTIMONY

green press
INITIATIVE

Lantern Books is committed to preserving ancient forests and natural resources. We elected to print this title on 100% post-consumer recycled paper, processed chlorine-free. As a result, for this printing, we have saved:

6 Trees (40' tall and 6-8" diameter)
2,279 Gallons of Wastewater
4 million BTUs of Total Energy
293 Pounds of Solid Waste
549 Pounds of Greenhouse Gases

Lantern Books made this paper choice because our printer, Thomson-Shore, Inc., is a member of Green Press Initiative, a nonprofit program dedicated to supporting authors, publishers, and suppliers in their efforts to reduce their use of fiber obtained from endangered forests.

For more information, visit www.greenpressinitiative.org

Environmental impact estimates were made using the Environmental Defense Paper Calculator. For more information visit: www.edf.org/papercalculator

BY THE WORD OF
THEIR TESTIMONY

The Journey of a Priest

MURCHADH
Ó MADAGÁIN

LANTERN BOOKS • NEW YORK

A Division of Booklight Inc.

2009
Lantern Books
128 Second Place, Garden Suite
Brooklyn, NY 11231

Printed in the United States of America

Cover designer: John Tymkiw

Library of Congress Cataloging-in-Publication Data

Ó Madagáin, Murchadh.
By the word of their testimony : the journey
of a priest / Murchadh Ó Madagøin.
p. cm.
Includes bibliographical references.
ISBN 978-1-59056-119-5 (alk. paper)
1. Ó Madagáin, Murchadh. 2. Priests—Biography.
3. Catholic Church—Clergy—Biography. I. Title.
BX4705.O13A3 2009
282.092—dc22
[B]
2008049178

And they have conquered him
by the blood of the Lamb
and by the word of their testimony,
for they did not cling to life
even in the face of death.
Rejoice then you heavens,
and those who dwell in them.
(Revelations 12:11–12)

ACKNOWLEDGMENTS

I WOULD LIKE TO ACKNOWLEDGE several people who helped me make this book possible. As always, thanks to my family, who are an ongoing source of strength. Thanks to John McCarthy for his encouragement and inspiration. Special thanks to Regina Collins for carefully going over the whole text and making various suggestions and criticisms. Thanks also to Ian and Nóirín, JoAnne and Leo, Sharon, and many other friends for their continual faith in me.

◑ CONTENTS

Chapter One

 COMING HOME TO GOD

EARLY DAYS

I WAS BORN IN 1969 in a suburb of Dublin called Dún Laoghaire, which is right on the sea. I don't remember an awful lot from our time in Dublin, since we moved to Galway on the west coast when I was just six years old. Strangely enough, most of my childhood memories are rather fearful ones. I had a vivid imagination and was easily frightened. Two particular events speak for themselves. During my first year of school (I was about five years old at the time), there was construction work being done on the building. In the schoolyard there was a fire, probably to heat tar or burn rubbish. When I became aware of the fire I was convinced that it was only a matter of time before the whole school went up in flames and me with it. I did my best to warn the teacher, but she told me there was nothing to worry about. However, I wasn't so sure and so I asked to be allowed to go to the toilet and then stole out of the school by myself. I was going to survive! Now having escaped from the fire and certain death, the only problem was that I'd never made my own way home from school before. I'm not sure how I did it, but somehow I found my way back to our house. Having made the great journey home, I was disgusted to find that instead of my parents congratulating me on my sensible escape, they brought me straight back to the school!

Another similar incident happened at a party. One day during the same year I was brought to the house of a school friend. My sister was there too, so at least I wasn't alone. For some reason I decided that I didn't like this party and I wanted to go home. The only problem was that I'd only just arrived and so there was no way I could go home again. So my creative young mind devised a plan. I told my friend Ruairí that we'd play hide-and-seek. I'd go and hide in the garden, but I warned him to give me plenty of time to hide well. Then he'd come and try to find me. So I went out into the garden and promptly climbed the wall and set out for home. This time I'd absolutely no idea how to get home, but that wasn't going to stop me. All I can remember from this adventure was that I stopped to ask a postman how to get to York Road, where we lived. With a puzzled look on his face he explained to me which way to go, and off I went. When I finally arrived home I found a police motor-bike in the front drive and a huge policeman saying into the phone, "It's OK, we've found him." My unfortunate parents weren't happier for these events. My mother wasn't impressed with the postman either. She couldn't figure out why he wasn't more suspicious of a five-year-old asking for directions home!

In 1975, we moved west, as my father had just been made professor of the Irish language in University College, Galway. Galway was a liberating experience for me, as it was a much smaller and safer town. As a result I had greater freedom to wander around the estate I lived in, and within a couple of years I was allowed to cycle into the town by myself. This was something special, particularly for an adventurous (though still nervous) young boy like me.

Being from a Catholic family, my siblings and I were brought to mass on Sundays and went to Catholic schools, in name at least. At that time in Ireland it would have been difficult not to go to a Catholic school, as just about all schools were Catholic. I made my first Holy Communion when I was seven and then my Confirmation when I was twelve, as nearly all children did at the time. I hardly remember either of these events, except that I got to wear lovely new clothes. I knew that both of these celebrations were very special, but I don't recall them being particularly "spiritual" in any sense. One strange thing that I do remember was a prayer that I found myself offering to God at a young age. I seemed to have a sense that maybe I'd lose my way at some stage, and I used to pray, "God please know that I love you, even if I seem to forget all about you." Perhaps it was a kind of premonition of what was to come.

LOSING MY RELIGION

During my teens, like many of my peers, I began to lose interest in religion. I was bored with mass and didn't understand what was going on. I always had respect for it, but I began to think I must be a hypocrite, since I seemed to spend a lot of the time dreaming, mostly about girls. Eventually I decided that I'd not go to mass anymore, although I never felt totally happy about this within myself. Perhaps it was just guilt, but either way I was still not convinced either that I should or shouldn't be there. I remember a friend of mine called Michael announcing that he had now taken to "going for a pint" (as the Irish call going for a drink) instead of going to mass, although he wasn't letting his parents in on this as yet.

I found my years in secondary school (high school) difficult and the only things that kept me going were friends and music. I used to listen to music for hours on end. It was my escape. The subjects in school didn't interest me and being very sensitive I found the strictness of the school oppressive. No doubt the teachers were doing their best to deal with teenage boys, but I was never happy there. One of the best days of my life was when I received my final exam results and realized that I was completely finished with secondary school. I never wanted to darken its doors again. Our home was quite strict, too, and it seemed to me that I was always being asked if I was working enough. Naturally, my parents were concerned for us to do well for ourselves, but as a teenager this can feel very stifling. I was going through all the usual struggles of hormones and trying to date girls at this time, which of course was both exciting but also difficult, since at this stage of your life you don't really know what is going on. I also began working weekends in a nightclub in town. I think if my parents had known half of the things that were going on in that club, they'd never have let me work there! However, it was a great experience for me and probably a good education too. If nothing else it was a good insight into the seedier side of life. Sex, drugs, and rock 'n' roll were all around me and I was getting paid! I used to go out a lot myself as well, usually about three nights a week. A lot of my friends were heavy drinkers, though I never drank much myself. It was quite normal for some of them to put away up to fourteen pints on a night out, and even with this amount of alcohol they wouldn't be drunk. The body's tolerance continues to amaze me. I was more interested in girls, though I didn't seem to have much success with relationships, but it certainly wasn't for lack of effort.

DEATH

Early in January 1988, when I was about to turn nineteen, I received a phone call from a classmate to say that a very dear friend of mine by the name of Michael Feeney had been killed the day before in a car accident. I was crippled with shock. His family knew me well and when I came to the house to see Michael's body laid out in the coffin, I fainted with fright. It was my first close experience of death and a deeply painful one. While I believed in God and the after life, this suddenly brought up many questions for me. At that stage of your life death isn't something you think about much, as the world is your oyster and you feel immortal. But now there seemed to be a dark cloud beyond which I wasn't permitted to see, blocking out all the answers to my questions. I was in college at the time, studying marketing, though I really had no idea what I wanted to do with my life.

That summer I went to New York. I got a J-1 visa that enabled students to work legally in the United States for the summer. In order to get this visa you needed a letter from someone in the States saying that they'd look after you financially should anything happen to you. I wrote to some distant relatives explaining this situation to them. Not only did they give me the letter I needed, but they insisted I come and stay with them as well, which was not only more than I expected but a welcome relief. I'm sure it was even more of a relief for my parents who no doubt were worried for their enthusiastic nineteen-year-old son, heading off to New York on his own.

I'd never been to America before, though most of the TV programs we watched were American, so at least I had a fair idea what to expect. It was very exciting to suddenly be in this great country that I'd seen so much of. For our first night there all students on the J-1 visa program had to stay in the YMCA on 32nd street in Manhattan, so that we could be given a basic introduction to America and what to watch out for. I still remember being quite surprised to find that even the security guards for this building were armed. Manhattan at that time was pretty rough, and I remember seeing a guy having his bag snatched right beside me on the first night.

During the summer I stayed with a relative called Jim Milligan on Long Island. He was a marvelous character who had worked as a lawyer all his life, and, at eighty-five years of age was still going to work every day. Jim and I got on very well and I think he was glad of the company. I got a job in a supermarket called the A&P, which was just thirty minutes walk from Jim's house. I really enjoyed working there, especially with the language differences. The staff thought that some of my expressions were hilarious, and vice-versa. Once when I had to try and unblock part of a garbage compressor, I needed some extra light. So I said to the manager who was with me, "Do you have a torch?" He replied, "Merk" (which was what they called me), "This is the twentieth century. Here we use flashlights!" My expression had obviously brought up an image of me climbing into the garbage compressor with a big stick with flames coming out the top! Another man I worked with had a bad stammer and explained that he couldn't pronounce a name beginning with "M." I jokingly suggested that he call me Harry, and he did.

True to their reputation, my relatives on Long Island were very good to me and looked after my every need. They also introduced me to many more relatives in other parts of Long Island and New Jersey. All of them were so welcoming. Occasionally I went to mass, but this was mostly to keep my conscience at bay. I guess I still wasn't happy at the idea of abandoning my religion. However, I was searching. By the end of that summer I found myself thinking, "I have to find out more about this faith, or else quit altogether." I didn't want to just drift, as I had seen many others do. So I finished my adventure in America and came back to Ireland to continue my studies and try to figure out what to do with my life. My family weren't impressed that I returned with an American accent!

When I returned to Ireland at the end of the summer I came across a book in my room called *Power for Living* by Jamie Buckingham. I've no idea who put the book in my room, but it was literally on my desk. This book was a series of testimonies by different people who had discovered the power of God in their lives and the difference their faith made to them. I was fascinated. At the end of the book it said something like, "If you really want God to be a part of your life, invite him now in your own words to come into your life." So I did just that. I remember sitting on the end of my bed and saying, "God, if you're really there, help me to find you." Then I put the book away and forgot all about it. I could never have imagined what was to follow.

A couple of weeks later a good friend of mine called Aidan told me that he had met a mutual friend of ours by the name of Louise on a bus from Dublin. She'd been to a place called Medjugorje (about which I write in Chapter Three) and was now, in my friend's words, "all religious and holy." Now I knew Louise was from a similar kind of background to me and I was really curious to know what had happened to her. So, being the over confident young man that I was, I called around to her house to ask her about it. The fact that I thought she was very attractive was also a major incentive to visit her.

I'd heard of Medjugorje but knew little or nothing about it. While she was there, Louise had had a reawakening of her faith and was now bursting to tell anyone who would listen. The problem, she had found, was how to bring up this topic in conversation. To her surprise, I called to her house and straightaway asked her to tell me about Medjugorje and what had happened. Strangely, I cannot remember anything about what she told me, but she spoke for an hour and a half and I was amazed. Before I left that evening she asked me if I'd be interested in coming to a prayer meeting in town the following Monday. She explained that it was simply a group of young people who came together to pray the Rosary and sing hymns for a while. I wasn't so enthusiastic about this. I wasn't inclined to think that meeting to pray the Rosary and sing hymns could be up to much. However, Louise was smarter than I and she got a friend of hers called Sharon, whom I had eyes for, to invite me as well. Naturally, I went!

PRAYER GROUPS

When I arrived at this meeting, which was held in a family home, I felt somewhat out of place; but I was curious to see perhaps fifty or sixty people there around my own age who seemed to be quite ordinary. They began by singing a hymn, and then they prayed the Rosary. After the Rosary, they sang several more hymns and then they praised God out loud and some people also prayed "in tongues." Now this "praying in tongues" definitely got my attention. I'd heard of this phenomenon once before, but had never witnessed it directly. I later discovered that the gift of tongues is a gift of the Holy Spirit given to almost anyone who is open to it. It is mentioned many times in the Acts of the Apostles and also in some of St. Paul's letters.[1] What happens is that the person who receives this gift has the ability to speak in a language they're not familiar with, and strangely enough they don't know exactly what they're saying. It's tempting to think that this is probably just gibberish, but every so often God will bring someone along who happens to understand the "tongue" in which another person is praying, and will often be able to confirm that it isn't something made up. I later witnessed this several times myself.

It happened once that I was at a seminar on the Holy Spirit, where people were being taught about the reality of God's Spirit and how that Spirit can and will make our faith alive if we are open to it. There was a man who was very skeptical of everything, but especially of the gift of tongues. Toward the end of the seminar a woman beside him began to pray in tongues and he recognized it as a form of Greek that he'd studied years before. It was the Greek in which the New Testament was written (known as *Koine*) and he also knew that this woman didn't know a word of that language. He later gave witness to this himself and how it had helped him to believe in what was happening.

This prayer meeting was my first experience of the gift of tongues. Some people read passages from the Bible and someone gave a short teaching on what it meant. Everyone sang together and prayed for the power of God's Spirit to come upon all who were present and make them new again in their faith and speak to them. After praying to the Holy Spirit for a few minutes, everyone went quiet. I wasn't aware that anything really happened, but something felt very different, though I couldn't say what it was, except that I was attracted to what happened. There was an almost tangible presence of the Divine. Then different people shared thoughts or ideas that they believed God was saying to them, or sometimes a passage from the Bible. Finally some time was given to prayers for different needs and we finished with a hymn. What intrigued me most though was the fact that obviously, all these young people were quite sincere in what they were doing. None of them had to be in that room. They were there because they wanted to be and it was obvious they had something very real, which I realized I wanted myself. They knew God in a way that I didn't.

In the weeks that followed I continued to go to the meetings each Monday night. These young people, many of whom I'm still in regular contact with, taught me how to pray. They showed me that it was good to begin the day by thanking God for it; by reading part or parts of the Bible—the inspired word of God—and also by asking God for His blessing. I began to do just that, spending about ten minutes in the morning praying to God.

Several weeks after I began going to the "Monday night meeting," as it was called, the group held what is known as a "Life in the Spirit" seminar, which I mentioned earlier. This is a series of seven or eight talks where the teachings focus on the reality of the Holy Spirit and the power of the Spirit in our lives in a very practical way. Each evening we had the prayer meeting as usual, but the talks would be focused on this topic. People would also give their story, or "testimony," which was always impressive, even when the story was quite simple. One man called John M. recalled how his youth had been wasted on drink and drugs. When he was thirteen he had been involved in a bad car accident. He suffered head injuries, which caused him continuous trouble for years. A psychiatrist told him that he'd always have bad concentration and an inability to love. He started drinking at the age of fourteen and by sixteen had dropped out of school. He also stopped practicing his faith around the same time and began to live more and more recklessly. He was constantly getting drunk and having blackouts. Over the next ten years he worked in Spain, England, and America. He drank a lot and dabbled in drugs. Eventually, working in Central Park in New York, he was earning a lot of money, but blowing most of it on alcohol and drugs. He began to wonder what his life was all about.

Around this time one of his brothers went to visit him and was very distressed to see the state that John was in. He returned home and began praying intensely that John would recover his life. At the same time John started to visit a Franciscan church near Pennsylvania Station and to pray to Padre Pio (now St. Pio of Pietrelcina). Padre Pio was a Capuchin Franciscan priest, who had lived in Italy and died in 1968. He was famous for having various mystical gifts, but especially for having the "stigmata," or bleeding wounds of Christ, in his body. John had heard about this man through his grandmother and he began to ask for his help. He didn't understand who God was, but he could relate to Padre Pio. Through his intercession, something changed and John hasn't taken a drink since. John later returned to Ireland and after being invited to a prayer meeting, began to pray and attend mass again. His faith continued to grow and, in 2006, after being involved with prayer groups for many years, he set up a school of evangelization for young people in Ireland, the first of its kind. John was one of the first people to welcome me to the prayer meeting and he is still a very dear friend.

I found the "Life in the Spirit" seminar fascinating. I was hoping for some kind of new beginning in my faith, which was already starting to happen, but, I wondered, could all that I was being told about God really happen to me as well? I was hearing the stories of different people as they witnessed to how God had changed their lives, and how the Spirit guided them daily in different ways and gave them new insights into the mysteries of God, as well as new meaning and purpose. As I began to talk about what I was discovering, my family watched nervously hoping it wouldn't all end in disaster.

On the fifth night of the seminar we were told that people would pray with us individually for a "fresh outpouring of the Holy Spirit," which sounded very exciting, although I didn't really know what that meant. How could I know, not having experienced it before? When the long-awaited night came, I had prepared myself as well as I could and had prayed to God myself that He would bless me with the gift of his Spirit. As it happened I was also starting a part-time job the same evening and there was nothing I could do about it. The timing couldn't have been worse, or so I thought.

The meeting went ahead as usual and it came to the time to pray with each person for the much-anticipated "outpouring of the Holy Spirit." What would happen? What if nothing occurred, which is what I suspect my family were more worried about than anything else. That could have been the final blow to my faith. It was an understandable fear. Groups of two or three people began praying with each one of us, and the priest who was present, a holy Franciscan by the name of Fr. Des O'Malley, also went around and prayed with each one, just to be sure! I was watching the clock because I had to go out to start my new job, too. Finally, they came to me and prayed for several minutes. Nothing in particular seemed to happen, except I felt peaceful, though not exceptionally so. Then it was over and as people began to talk about what they had experienced I had to rush off to work. I couldn't even wait to hear what had happened to the others. I was so disappointed. However, as always, God was well ahead of me.

I went to my new part-time job in a corner shop and did my work. When I was finished I went home and later called a friend called Peter. Peter had heard I was going to the prayer meetings and he was also curious. The amazing thing was that when I was in his house and after I'd told him about the meeting that night, I *then* had an experience of the Holy Spirit. Suddenly I felt an extraordinary peace come over me, almost as if I'd been drugged, although I was fully in control of myself. I'd never experienced anything like this in my life and I was sure it had to be from God. It was too beautiful and powerful to be anything else. I just wanted to rest there, not moving, not speaking, just being still. One thing it showed me was that the Spirit was quite happy to wait until I was ready. No rushing to "fit God in." It was an experience I will never forget.

A NEW BEGINNING

In the days and weeks that followed, much more began to happen. First, I found I had a profound desire to be alone and pray. I was still studying marketing in a business college and I remember that even during lectures I had a strong desire to go and pray. I also discovered I wanted to spend much more time in prayer. The Scriptures began to speak to me in a way I could never have imagined. God seemed to be uttering each word to me personally and it made sense of the expression I'd often heard that the Scriptures are the "living word" of God. Another profound difference I noticed was that the mass, which I'd now started to attend again, also began to come alive. I began to listen to the words the priest prayed as though I'd never heard them before. It was all new and God was powerfully present.

At the weekly prayer meetings I shared my newfound faith and all the amazing things that God seemed to be doing in my life. I was so enthusiastic that I began to tell others about it, too. Many listened with interest, although I don't remember that many people came to the meetings because of what I said; but I didn't mind. I knew that something extraordinary had happened and no one could take that away.

In the weeks that followed, I also found myself praying in tongues. At first I was slow to believe that this gift could be given to me, but then I realized that I had to trust and believe that the strange words or phrases in my head weren't made up and I began to say them out loud. All of these occurrences have remained with me to this day, though naturally they don't seem as extraordinary anymore. This "conversion," as you might call it, happened when I was nineteen. I continued to go to the prayer meetings and, because I was also a musician, I had an opportunity to be more involved, since we sang a lot at these meetings and quite a few of us played music as well, which was very enjoyable.

MUNICH

The summer after I'd been in New York, I decided to visit Munich with two other friends called Peter and Padraig. They were also attendees of the same prayer group, so we had our faith in common at least, although not much else! We had left it too late to book a flight that was in any way affordable, so we set off for Munich over land. This was a gruelling thirty-six-hour journey, which I wouldn't recommend unless you're able to sleep easily on trains. We were headed for Munich because we'd heard that there were many well-paid jobs for students and many other Irish students were visiting as well. Both Peter and Padraig had studied German in college; of course, I'd opted for Spanish. Nonetheless, I was always game for a bit of adventure.

When we arrived we were quite exhausted. We'd figured that it would be easy enough to get work and a place to stay, but it turned out not to be quite so straightforward. Initially, we checked into a youth hostel and began looking for work. Naturally, we were more limited since I didn't speak any German. We asked everywhere we could, without success. On the third day, we had to leave the hostel and we chose to stay in a campsite. We went to buy a tent and sleeping bags, but failed to realize that in Germany everything closed at lunchtime on Saturday. It was now Saturday afternoon and we were stuck. On the main square called Marienplatz, we came across a group of Christians evangelizing through mime, dance, and individual witness. Peter said, "Let's see just how Christian these people are." I figured he meant we should ask them for help, but I didn't think it was such a good idea. Peter walked straight up to the group and started talking. He explained our situation and that we were Christians ourselves. To my amazement, Peter returned after a few minutes and announced that one couple—Torsten and Arianne—were willing to let us stay with them, for that night at least. Someone taking in three strangers was quite something, but they were people of faith and they lived it.

It turned out that we got on wonderfully well with Torsten and Arianne, and became great friends. We loved praying and sharing our own faith with them. We ended up staying with them for three weeks, which looking back, is embarrassing. However, they insisted and we didn't refuse since we'd have been in difficulty without them. Eventually, we got work in a factory outside Munich in a small village called Erdweg. Arianne and Torsten introduced us to many of their friends—who weren't Catholic, so it was slightly different—and we attended some of their prayer groups. We enjoyed meeting their friends, although not all of them were happy about the fact that we were Catholic and some were eager to point out where we were "wrong."

In spite of this, it was still a pleasure to meet them all. Through Arianne and Torsten's friends we discovered that one came from the village where we were about to start work. Having made some enquiries, we were told that an elderly couple had an upstairs apartment they were happy to rent to us. We were thrilled. The couple let us have this apartment for next to nothing and the house was just five minutes walk from the factory. The factory made parts for Ford, BMW, and Jaguar cars, and so I spent the summer making ignition locks. It's probably the closest I'll ever get to owning a Jaguar! Other Irish students working in the same factory couldn't believe how we'd come to get accommodation right beside the factory. They had to travel by train to another town and were paying ten times the amount for rent. God had been so good to us.

AFTER TWO YEARS with the Galway prayer group I found myself in Dublin for a course on working in a travel agency. I stayed with my older brother in Killiney, a suburb about thirty minutes train-ride south of Dublin. Each day I traveled into the city for my course, and on the way back I'd often stop off in Dún Laoghaire, my birthplace. I used to enjoy going into St. Michael's church. Although I didn't recognize it as such, God was training me in the school of prayer and I'd often spend up to three hours at a time in prayer in the church, something I'd find very difficult to do now! This was a particular grace which God gave me at that time. Thanks to the prayer group, I'd learned the importance of reading sections from the Bible every day and listening to the word of God. I also used to pray the Rosary most days, reflecting on the mysteries of Jesus' life, just as we did in the meetings.

One evening I came into St. Michael's, hoping to attend mass. However, I got my times confused and when I arrived I discovered that mass had just ended. I decided to remain for a few minutes to pray anyway. On the opposite side of the church I noticed a light on over a confession box, indicating that a priest was present, and I felt a prompting to go to confession. It had only been a few days since I'd been to confession and I thought it would be ridiculous to go again, so I tried to put the idea out of my head. In spite of my efforts, however, the prompting I felt was so strong that I couldn't get it out of my mind, so I decided to act on it. I spent another few minutes trying to think of what I needed to confess and I went in.

I told the priest what was on my mind and that I had come back to my faith a few years before. I talked about the prayer group and how I missed the support of my friends in Galway, and so on. I also mentioned that I'd come to the church for mass but had confused the times. At the end of my confession the priest, Fr. Tom Fehily, said: "Do you know that you're a chosen soul?" I didn't know why he said this to me, but I found it strange and wasn't even sure what he meant. I suspect he recognized that God was already at work in me in an unusual way. He also told me that he normally never heard confessions during those hours, but that something had prompted him to go into the box after mass.

We were both sure that the Lord had intended us to meet. Fr. Tom then offered to give me Holy Communion, which I gratefully received. We became friends and he was to be the first one to introduce me to the Capuchin Franciscans, where I'd spend my first year of religious life. One day he suggested that we go and visit them. Always open to something different, I went along—even though I then had no interest in studying for religious life. But Fr. Tom could see further than I could. "One thing's for sure, Murchadh," he said, "you're not going to spend the rest of your life in a travel agency!" He was right. I used to call in to see him every so often and he was a great source of strength.

Fr. Tom also told me about some of his own unusual experiences of the spiritual life, which I always found fascinating. Once he'd been on a journey through the Dublin mountains with two other friends and they'd gotten quite lost. It was snowing and the roads were dangerous. At one stage they'd almost driven off the road down a steep ravine. As they sat in their vehicle wondering what to do a sports car sped up behind them and stopped. A man got out, tapped on the window of their car, and Fr. Tom rolled down the window. "Monsignor," said the man, "if you just go back down the road and take that last turn, you'll be alright." That was all he said, and just as quickly he left again. All three in the car said nothing but followed his instructions. That turn was the one they needed and brought them back to exactly where they were trying to go. But who was the man? How did he know where they needed to go and how did he know that Fr. Tom was a Monsignor? They felt sure he was sent by God.

Chapter Two

 RELIGIOUS LIFE

A CALLING

ABOUT A YEAR AFTER I came back to my faith, the idea
of priesthood began to cross my mind. However, not only
didn't the idea appeal to me, but it almost caused me to
panic, so I put it out of my head completely. Nevertheless,
two years later I began to feel a change within me. I wasn't
sure what this change was, except that I became more rest-
less and dissatisfied with my work at a travel agency in
Galway, going to the prayer group, and helping with "Life
in the Spirit" seminars and days of prayer. Each morning
before cycling to work I'd go to mass. This became essential to me. It was wonderful to begin each day by giving
time to God, listening to His Word, and receiving Jesus in
the Eucharist. Deep within me, I felt there had to be more
to life than what I was doing; yet I didn't know what else
that could be. I started to ask God for direction.

I received an opportunity to take a vacation in Florence,
where my sister was studying art. I began to think of visiting Assisi, home of the famous saints Francis and Clare,
which I knew was close to Florence. Since the director of

our prayer group was a Franciscan priest, it made me all the more curious to visit. The closer the time came for my holiday, the more I felt drawn to Assisi—that somehow I *had* to go there. I was still praying to God to give me direction. I spent ten wonderful days in Florence with my sister; it was my first time in Italy and I was overwhelmed by its extraordinary beauty, the Italians' wonderful sense of style, and the breathtaking art. I also ended up traveling to Assisi, where I prayed to St. Francis. Assisi is one of the most beautiful and inspiring places I've ever visited—virtually unchanged since St. Francis lived in the thirteenth century.

To this day I cannot recall whether it was there in Assisi, or just after I returned to Florence, that I had the following experience. One day, while I was praying, God gave me the answer I was looking for. I seemed to be outside myself and looking into my own heart. There I could "see" an invitation from God calling me to the priesthood. It wasn't something being forced on me, or a destiny I had no choice in; it was an open invitation, if ever I wanted to take it up. God so respects our freedom that He allows us to follow whatever path we choose, even if it means rejecting him. This is an extraordinary truth, but a wonderful reminder of the respect that God has for the freedom He's given us. This unforgetable experience had a deep impact on me: God was inviting me to become a priest, if I was willing to respond.

When I returned to Ireland I went straight to Fr. Des O'Malley and told him that I felt that God was calling me to become a priest. Being the wise man he was, Fr. Des said that he was delighted, but that I should continue praying and turning the idea over in my mind. Of course, I wanted to become a priest the following day; thankfully, however, this isn't how it works! I did as Fr. Des suggested and prayed for guidance to know if this was really what God was calling me to. At this stage, I'd left the travel agency to become a salesman in a jewelry store, which I thoroughly enjoyed and seemed to be good at.

After a few months I began talking to priests in the Capuchin Friars and the Franciscan Friars (both branches of the Franciscans). Since Fr. Des was a Franciscan himself, I found myself more drawn to the Franciscans initially, but the Capuchins seemed to have a better program of formation and I was accepted by them. I began my studies in Carlow, a small town about ninety minutes south of Dublin. I was thrilled, although I found it difficult to leave my friends from the prayer group in Galway. We'd developed a good friendship and had wanted this time to last forever.

During the three years with the prayer group in Galway, I'd learned a lot about Christianity, and had had a wonderful re-introduction to my faith. We'd given "Life in the Spirit" seminars throughout the west of Ireland and in doing so some wonderful things had occurred, such as many people being renewed and enthused in their faith. We'd also been blessed with Fr. Des, who was experienced and put up with no nonsense. If some of us began to get carried away with ideas about God "speaking" to us, he'd be quick to put a stop to it. I learned a lot from Fr. Des and I'm grateful for his example. He had a gift of being able to be in the background and yet keeping things on track. While prayer groups can be a great help to people, they also lend themselves to the kind of emotional highs and spiritual flights of fancy that can cause a lot of damage. They need to be carefully guided.

A YOUNG RELIGIOUS

The year I spent with the Capuchins was a wonderful one: I don't think I'd ever laughed as much. I admired thier great sense of family. (Years later, after I'd become a diocesan priest, I visited a remote Capuchin friary in Slovakia, and the atmosphere was exactly the same.) Throughout the year, our director Fr. Eddie Dowling brought us to all the different Capuchin houses in Ireland and showed us what the order was about. This was to be my "breaking in" year. Like many people, I had a very romantic idea as to what the religious life should and shouldn't be; and I was going to be disappointed with what I saw, because it wasn't as "extreme" as it should be. My idealistic notions of religious life were brought to earth with a crash; but it was something I needed to go through. I needed to become more realistic about the religious life: the reality of dealing with ordinary people, who are weak and sinful, just like the rest of humanity. While I thoroughly enjoyed the year with the Capuchins, by the end I felt I was in the wrong place, although I was still quite sure that God was calling me to be a priest. I felt more drawn to work in the west of Ireland and believed a little more independence would suit me better than community life.

One weekend in the spring we visited Creeslough Friary, at one of the most northerly points of Ireland. I walked the friary's beautiful grounds and continued to ask God what I should do next, as I was sure at this stage that I wouldn't stay with the Capuchins. I thought of all the different religious orders and where I might go, but I couldn't think of any that held a particular attraction for me. It was then that I felt the Lord saying to me, "Think about what it is you want to do as a priest, rather than what order you want to be with." So I did just that. I then realized that I wanted to work in my home diocese of Galway, with more independence to live the kind of life I felt God calling me to, and serve the people as a priest. It suddenly seemed obvious that the place for me was the diocese of Galway. After some interviews, I was accepted by the diocese and that September I continued my studies in the national seminary of Maynooth, from which over twelve thousand priests have been ordained since it was founded in 1795.

One of the great benefits of attending the prayer meetings in Galway for three years was that I'd had a direct experience of the spiritual, which made it very real to me. It had raised many questions, which I now had an opportunity to explore through theological studies. I discovered that I loved theology and was good at it, as well. My time with the prayer group had also taught me the importance of a steady prayer life, regular reading of Scripture, and making use of God's wonderful gift of confession to help us begin again. I'd no idea what a huge support this would be to me in the seminary; it provided me with a great foundation from which to study for the priesthood.

The seminary offered a sound, all-round "formation"— the education and training as a priest—but could do no more. As we were frequently reminded, it was up to us whether we engaged with that formation or not. I spent five tough but enjoyable years in Maynooth, where we were pushed hard and provided with a great education in the broadest sense of the word. I greatly admired the priests and laypeople who taught us; they exemplified admirably people who dedicated themselves to God, serving as best they could through whatever gifts they had. I also respected my fellow students in my class and seminary; many had already worked and studied in other areas before formation, and we were all quite different. I've great respect for anyone willing to give as they did.

PRISON

As part of our training, we engaged in various kinds of "pastoral" work—such as teaching, visiting the sick, and working with refugees, etc. For two years, I went into Dublin once a week to see prisoners in a maximum security prison called Arbour Hill. This was a worthwhile but humbling experience and opened up my mind to a different side of life. John (not his real name) was serving a life sentence for murder and Michael (also not his real name) was in for three years for a sex crime. I got on very well with both men; because we were in the prison for a "spiritual" visit, we were allowed visit the prisoners in their own cells. I'm sure they enjoyed the distraction of having someone visit to break the monotony of each day. John was very funny and I always came out feeling that he'd done far more for me than I had for him. His crime was tragic, one he deeply regretted. What was extraordinary was that thirty seconds in either direction and he'd never have met the person he killed. Such bizarre circumstances make you realize the fragility of our choices. In spite of the seriousness of his crime, I was always struck by his sincerity and goodness.

From visiting both men and listening to their stories, I became very aware that it wouldn't take much for any of us to be in prison likewise. You often hear people talking about prisoners as if they were monsters from the day of their birth; the truth is that many are victims of their dysfunctional background. If I'd grown up in similar circumstances, it's quite likely I would be in prison for similar crimes. Now when I hear of someone in prison and hear people shouting that the sentence should be longer and more severe, I think of my visits to Arbour Hill. It isn't a place I'd wish to spend even one night.

SCANDALS

In the summer of 1992, I was accepted by the Capuchin Franciscans. At the same time, the first major scandal broke in the Church in Ireland. Bishop Eamon Casey of Galway resigned over a relationship he'd had with a woman; he'd fathered a child and Church money had been misused. This came as a huge shock to most people, as nothing like this had happened in the Irish Church before, at least not that we were aware of. The Church was far too "respectable" for this; indeed, that was part of the problem. The scandals of pedophilia that followed made the Casey affair look tame. The media had a field day and drip-fed the public with story after story, giving the impression that every other priest in the country was corrupt, perverted, and not to be trusted in any way.

Trust had been broken and terrible harm done. The reality was that less than three percent of the clergy were involved in any kind of scandals. It was still three percent too many and inexcusable, but it's important to keep the numbers in perspective. The sad and dangerous weakness that some men suffer from is one of the tragic sicknesses of humanity—it's a human problem rather than one of the priesthood, although it was portrayed as the latter. We're indebted to the media in helping bring this abuse to light; it was a cancer under the surface, doing untold damage to the people we were meant to be serving. While the numbers carrying out the abuse were few, everyone became suspect; this in turn caused great suffering for many good priests and religious trying to get on with their work.

The scandals were a very difficult experience for those of us studying to be priests. It made us think carefully about what we were doing and why we were in the seminary. We were left under no illusions as to what we were facing—that we'd be going out into a very different Ireland than our predecessors. In some ways, we were strengthened. We were forced to ask whether we believed in our faith or not. If we believed, and we did, then the scandals were a great tragedy, but had nothing to do with the faith we wanted to help pass on. Most of us persevered. At the same time, these tragedies brought about a kind of purification in the Church that was badly needed—and isn't over yet. Ireland was almost completely Catholic in name, but the reality was that many people weren't at all Catholic and had little or no interest in the Church. The result was that we had large numbers going to church, but not so many who took their faith seriously. After the scandals, many people dropped away, but those who remained became more fervent. In fact, these scandals have left a smaller but healthier Church.

Cardinal Joseph Ratzinger (later Pope Benedict XVI) was once asked in an interview about the scandals and corruption in the Church, and how they could occur in an institution that was supposed to be holy. The cardinal replied by pointing to the parable of the wheat and the darnel (cf. Matthew 13:24–30). In the parable, an enemy sows weeds among the wheat. When the servants notice and offer to pull them out, the master tells them to leave the weeds, lest pulling them out damage the wheat as well. Ratzinger explained that the reality was that there would always be a certain amount of corruption and evil in our world and there was nothing that could be done. We should deal with what we could, of course, but we'd also have to bear some problems, as it wasn't possible to make everything perfect. Likewise, because there are problems in our Church or society doesn't mean that God isn't present, or that He cannot work in an imperfect situation. On the contrary, as the Lord said to St. Paul, "My strength is at its best in weakness" (2 Corinthians 12:9). Not only is our weakness not a problem, but in fact it's the key to God's power working through us, as I'll explain in more detail later. This is one of the paradoxes of our faith.

Time in the seminary flew by and before I knew it I was ordained a priest on the 14th June, 1998, at the age of twenty-nine. It was an extremely wet month, even for the west of Ireland, but on both the day of my ordination and the one after, when I celebrated my first mass, to my delight and to everyone's amazement there wasn't a cloud in sight. The day after, it was raining again.

Chapter Three

 MEDJUGORJE

THE EVENTS

THE PRAYER GROUP I'd been involved with before entering the seminary had started directly as a result of the events
in Medjugorje²—a small village in Bosnia-Herzegovina (former Yugoslavia), nestled between hills (which is what the
name means). For the most part it is farming country with
extensive vineyards, and before 1981 was virtually unheard
of. However, on 24th June, 1981, two local children saw a
lady hovering above the ground on the hill known as Podbrodo, beckoning them to come closer. Terrified, they fled.
Later that same evening they returned with several other
children. Again they saw the lady, who said to them, "peace,
peace, peace." In the days and weeks that followed six children continued to claim to see Mary, the Mother of God,
or Gospa, as she's called in the local language. The children were Mirjana Dragicevic Soldo, Ivanka Ivankovic Elez,
Ivan Dragicevic, Marija Pavlovic, Jacov Colo, and Vicka
Ivankovic. For years after this, these visionaries claimed that
Gospa continued to appear to them every day. As of 2008,
three of them report having these visions on a daily basis.

I've read a lot of literature on the events of Medjugorje, both "for" and "against." Many people have tried to convince me that what occurred is true and many others that it's a hoax. Since there are ample books describing in detail what happened, I won't go into detail about it here; instead, I'll describe what I've heard and seen personally.

As I mentioned, the prayer group that returned me to my faith started as a direct result of Medjugorje. One young lady called Sandra felt inspired to begin a prayer group in Galway; she along with her family began to pray the Rosary together in their home. Others joined, and the group began to grow. After some time, there were so many people that the group decided to split into one for younger and another for older people. Both groups continued to expand and large numbers started coming each week to pray. Many who went to these meetings had either been to Medjugorje, or ended up visiting because of others' enthusiasm. A huge number that I know personally either came back to their faith or believed in God for the first time—as a direct result of what was happening in Medjugorje.

These "conversions" weren't short-lived bursts of enthusiasm. Most of the people I got to know through the prayer group are still trying to live their faith seriously. Indeed, from this prayer group alone came several vocations. Colette Hayden and Gabriel Grealish—both very dear friends of mine and both qualified accountants—entered the Poor Clares.[3] Two vocations to the priesthood also came from the same group: my own and that of Fr. Sean Forde, a practicing solicitor who became a Carmelite priest and is now working in England. Several others also tried religious life for a time, but later decided it wasn't for them. Apart from the vocations, many people married others from the same group. They now have their own families and are passing on their faith to their children. I'm still in regular contact with many of these people and they've been a great support to me as a priest. Today, in Galway alone there's a whole network of people trying to live their faith seriously. Nearly all have been influenced by Medjugorje and many of them continue to go there on pilgrimage.

In spring 1989, I visited Medjugorje for the first time. By then, I'd been attending prayer meetings for seven months and I had a great desire to go to this place that everyone seemed so excited about. I prayed that the opportunity would arise, and it did. It was a strange experience. Everyone seemed to be praying the Rosary, going to daily mass and confession. It was certainly not what I was used to seeing at home. Because of the huge numbers of pilgrims many local people were happy to look after the visitors through guesthouses. In 1989, the village was still quite undeveloped. I was impressed by the sincerity and generosity of the people, who had very little, but were more than happy to share it with the pilgrims.

Each morning at ten o'clock, a mass was held for English-speaking pilgrims. The church was always packed to capacity and a large number of priests from all over the world celebrated mass together. The preaching was powerful and everyone seemed to come away renewed and encouraged in their faith. I always felt the message preached was to the point and what we all needed to hear, while the priests spoke with a conviction that you didn't often find at home. The main event of each day was the Rosary and mass in the evening. This consisted of the Joyful and Sorrowful mysteries of the Rosary followed by mass in the local language, but an international mass for all the pilgrims. The Gospel was read in every language of the priests at the altar. During the Rosary and before the mass, confessions were heard—and it was inspiring to see the long lines of people going to confession in all the different languages. After the mass the Glorious Mysteries of the Rosary were also prayed. Little did I know that nine years later, I'd return as an ordained priest.

Apart from the official daily events—such as mass and various talks put on for the pilgrims—people visited "Apparition Hill" or Podbrodo, where Our Lady first appeared to the children. People would also climb the bigger hill called Krizevac, or "Cross Mountain"—so called because of a big cross erected on top in 1933. Everywhere you went you'd find people walking and praying the Rosary, or spending quiet time alone. I only saw two unusual things. The first was on the day I arrived. Many of us were walking along the road to Podbrodo in the dark and several people began pointing to the cross on Krizevac, which was lit up as though it were a neon sign. I thought it was pretty, but took no more notice of it. It was only the following day when I climbed the mountain myself and realized that the fifteen-foot-high cross was made of concrete and there were no lights near it that it occurred to me that I'd seen anything out of the ordinary.

The second unusual thing I witnessed was on one of my later trips. Many people had spoken of seeing the sun "dance" in the sky. One particular evening I noticed that many people were looking at the sun (understandably priests there strongly discourage this). I also looked out of curiosity. To my surprise, it was possible to look at the sun and see what seemed like a disk rolling around within the disk shape of the sun. I watched it for some time and was intrigued, but that was the extent of the experience. Other people have had strange signs, but I never noticed anything else, nor was I concerned about it. What most amazed me, and continues to impress me, was to see so many people devoutly attending mass and going to confession.

My first few visits to Medjugorje occurred before I began to study for the priesthood. Each time, I found myself returning home with new energy and hope. When I got an opportunity to return on pilgrimage, I was a deacon (an ordained minister of the Church, who usually serve in this ministry for about a year). I asked myself whether the fact that I'd studied theology would make me see things differently, as it had changed my faith and given me a different perspective. However, what I noticed at Medjugorje was that the emphasis was as it should be: on daily mass, prayer, and confession, and not only on supernatural phenomena. This has always impressed me about Medjugorje. It has become what you might call a "school of prayer." People come away with a new sense of the need to make daily prayer a part of their lives and begin to take the call to conversion seriously.

THE MESSAGE

What is the message of the apparitions? The children tell us that from the beginning of the visions Our Lady emphasized the need for prayer, especially prayer for peace. She told them that people are living as though God doesn't exist and that we must turn back to God. If we continue to live as we are, she said, we will destroy ourselves.

A cursory reading of the papers shows how true this is. We must begin to take God seriously, pray and fast, read the Scriptures, and to live God's commandments. In a way, this is nothing new. Anywhere the Mother of God has appeared, she's more or less given the same message: We cannot live without God and we need to turn back to Him.

It's the message of the Gospels. I heard someone describe Medjugorje as "a place where Our Lady is spoon-feeding us the Gospels," which I think is a very accurate description. The Blessed Mother is acting as a signpost to God; the visions are not about her, but simply pointing us in the right direction, just as any mother does for her children. If the children go astray, the mother picks them up and puts them back on the right path.

WHAT THE CHURCH SAYS

To date the Church hasn't made any definitive statement about Medjugorje, except for the following from the Yugoslav Conference of Bishops in 1991:

> The Bishops, from the very beginning, have been following the events of Medjugorje through the Bishop of the diocese (Mostar), the Commission of the Bishop (Mostar) and the Commission of the Yugoslav Bishops' Conference on Medjugorje.
>
> On the basis of the investigations to date, it cannot be affirmed that one is dealing with supernatural apparitions and revelations.[4]

Fr. René Laurentin, a leading Church theologian who specializes in Marian apparitions, points out in his book *Medjugorje Testament*,[5] that this text means that the supernatural hasn't been established (yet), since the investigation is ongoing. It doesn't mean that the non-supernatural character of the events has been established. The difference is subtle, but important: the supernatural character is neither established nor excluded.

As an individual priest, I'm in no position to make any kind of judgment, as this is well beyond the ability of any individual. However, the Church investigates such events carefully and thoroughly and no doubt will make whatever judgment it sees fit at the appropriate time. Meanwhile, many parishes and even dioceses are attributing their renewal to this extraordinary place. It is for us priests to continue to minister to the spiritual needs of people as best we can, while at the same time remaining faithful to the guidance of the Church.

Personally I believe in what has happened there simply from the fruits that it has borne: the many who've come back to their faith; the number of prayer groups that have sprung up all over Ireland and in many other parts of the world; the abundance of vocations to the priesthood and religious life that have been inspired by it. I've met many men studying to be priests who attribute their vocation directly to Medjugorje. I'd find it hard to believe that any kind of hoax, no matter how elaborate, could produce the kind of conversions that have take place, not to mention the many vocations and new communities that have sprung up because of what occurred in that small village nigh on thirty years ago.

Chapter Four

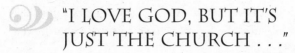 "I LOVE GOD, BUT IT'S
JUST THE CHURCH . . ."

DISILLUSION

ONE OF THE THINGS, people frequently say to me is, "Father, it's not that I don't love God, but it's just the Catholic Church. . . ." The comment points to the often understandable disillusionment that many people have with regard to the Church. They may have had a bad experience from someone they expected would show them compassion. Or, having come through a painful separation and all the emotional trauma that goes with it, a person might have finally found someone else who loved them and were just beginning to get back on their feet, only to be told they couldn't receive Holy Communion because they were in a second marriage without having gotten an annulment from the first. The very organization they expected to care for them, seemed to be turning its back.

I understand this disillusionment, and in some ways I'm surprised there aren't more disillusioned people. No doubt such feelings are partly because individuals come to priests when they're down or upset and we don't always say the right thing. The result can be that people withdraw into their shell and begin to distance themselves from the Church they grew up in. It's sad, but it's also the reality. Nonetheless, the more of these impossible situations that I come up against, the more I become convinced of the mercy of God—because of some of the extraordinary things that happen, often at the most unexpected times. That is what we call "grace."

MIRACLES IN LOURDES

For two summers in a row, I spent several weeks working in Lourdes hearing confessions. People are surprised when I tell them that this was one of the most wonderful experiences of my priesthood, as they cannot imagine anything more boring than listening to people's confessions for hours on end. However, they don't realize what takes place in the confessional. For me, it was an education in the mercy of God.

People from all over the English-speaking world would come and confess their sins—some that were very serious. Many people hadn't been for years or even decades and carried terrible burdens of shame and guilt because of a mistake they'd made in the past. The miracles that I saw daily—and they were just as real as any physical occurrences—were the healings that took place in those people. You could physically see the difference in their faces when they realized that they were forgiven and able to make a new beginning. It's a great privilege to be one of the instruments that God uses to bring His mercy to people in this way.

I also found it consoling, because having listened to people from all over the world, I realized that all of us, no matter what culture we're from, are struggling with the same problems. We're all sinners and we're all in pain: this is the human race. We're sick and in need of healing—healing that is waiting for us, if only we'd reach out and take it. I often think that if more people could hear what goes on in confession they'd actually be very consoled, because they'd realize how we're all struggling with our fallen nature.

In fact, I found it astonishing that so many people came to confession at all, considering all the bad press—sometimes well-deserved—the Church received. What made thousands of people come to confession, against all the odds? Grace. The loving power of God at work in a way we cannot see and certainly don't understand, opening doors where no one thought it was possible.

We don't often see this side of the Church because it's hidden. The confessional is one of the many places where God continually heals and consoles people, but hardly anyone is aware of it and it rarely makes the papers. This is another reason why I love the Church and see the power of God at work there so much—the most beautiful work that takes place in the Church is unseen. God ministers to His people through His priests and through all of His people as well. It's usually only scandals that make headlines, but there are countless miracles taking place all the time. That's also why the Church is still here; it's the vessel that God uses to minister to His people on Earth.

I was once asked whether priests discuss with each other all the things that people tell them in confession. To answer this question I'm reminded of something that was said to us when we were studying to be priests: "What do you do if you're brought to court and ordered to divulge something that you were told in confession?" Sometimes this might happen if in confession a priest has been given information regarding a serious crime. The answer was what I hoped it would be: "You keep your mouth shut and go to prison if you have to, rather than break the seal of confession." The "seal" of confession, as it's called, is the secrecy that the priest is bound to observe and it's considered something very sacred. No priest is allowed to break that seal under any circumstances and we take it very seriously.[6] In fact, if a priest deliberately breaks the seal of confession he's automatically excommunicated (cut off) from the Church. Of course, at times priests will discuss with each other some difficult moral dilemmas that come up in confession, but it will be done completely anonymously.

BUT WHY SHOULD WE LISTEN TO THE CHURCH ANYWAY?

In order to answer this question properly we retrace our footsteps all the way back to the beginning of the Church itself.

[Jesus said to Peter]: "You are Peter and on this rock I will build my Church. And the gates of the underworld can never overpower it. I will give you the keys of the kingdom of Heaven: whatever you bind on earth will be bound in heaven; whatever you loose on earth will be loosed in heaven." (Matthew 16:18–19)

Since Jesus is God, why on earth would he have given His authority to ordinary people; this is what we believe this piece of Scripture means. There are several points worth noting here. First, while God works through ordinary, sinful human beings, it is always *His* Church, which is why we say the Church is "holy." It belongs to God and comes from God. Secondly, "the gates of the underworld can never overpower it." Anyone would be forgiven for thinking that the underworld or "the powers of hell" have already overpowered the Church, but the truth is that they haven't and they never will, because they cannot. The reason for this is that the Church is from God and not of human origin; if it was, it would have disappeared centuries ago.

Think for a moment of the superpowers that have come and gone. The great Chinese and Egyptian dynasties, the Roman Empire, the European kingdoms, and so many others have risen and fallen. Most of these were far better organized than the Church, but their power was at best human; that of the Church is spiritual power from God. This is why it works in a way that continues to confound us.

There's a story told about Napoleon Bonaparte meeting the cardinal of Paris. "I will destroy the Vatican," Napoleon is said to have told the cardinal. "You won't be able," replied the cardinal. "We priests have been trying to destroy it for the last 1,800 years and we haven't been able to do it!" In spite of our best efforts to wreck it, as you might say, the Church endures—after centuries of sometimes terrible scandals, bad preaching, poor example, power trips, and people completely forgetting the meaning of their calling, the Church remains. To me this is the best "proof" that the Church is from God.

Thirdly, "I will give you the keys of the Kingdom. . . ." Jesus, the Son of God, entrusts his authority to Peter, the first pope and his successors. It isn't as if Jesus leaves the Church with Peter and then departs, leaving the latter to his own ideas. On the contrary, the reason Jesus does this is because God continues to work through Peter and his successors (the pope and bishops that we have with us right down to the present day). It's the power of God at work through human instruments. And Jesus promises to remain with them—to send them his Spirit to guide them and teach them all they need to know:

> When the Paraclete comes, whom I shall send to you from the Father, the Spirit of truth who issues from the Father, he will be my witness. And you too will be my witnesses because you have been with me from the beginning. (John 15:26)

> I still have many things to say to you but they would be too much for you to bear now. However, when the Spirit of truth comes he will lead you to the complete truth. . . . (John 16:12–13)

Before Jesus ascended to the Father he promised to send the Holy Spirit, who would teach and guide his Church, which is why we believe that the Church's teaching is from God and not from people. If it was from human beings then we could just take it or leave it, like any other opinion. However, if it comes from God—and we believe it does— then it's a completely different matter. It's why we struggle with it and try to live it as best we can, in spite of the fact that it often seems beyond us to do so.

Finally, "Whatever you bind on earth will be considered bound in heaven; whatever you loose on earth will be considered loosed in heaven." This tells us that the pope and his successors have the Lord's authority to act on earth in his name; to preach and teach, forgive sins, and to set free in his name. In modern English we might put it this way: "The decisions you make on earth will be recognized in heaven, *because I will be guiding those decisions so they are not merely human decisions.*" The bishops in the different dioceses all over the world are the successors of the

Apostles. We say that the pope is "the first among equals." The pope is the bishop of Rome, and he along with the college of bishops makes the decisions that guide us in our faith. The basic teaching of the faith never changes, but we are continually gaining new insights into what those teachings mean. As the years go by and people continue to pray and study theology, the Lord gives us ever deeper insights into his mysteries. That's why the Magisterium—or official teaching body of the Church—comes out with new documents on Church teaching every so often. It isn't that they keep changing their minds, rather that the Lord continually helps us to grow in understanding.

I've no doubt that one of the reasons why so many people develop a negative opinion of the Church is because more often than not we don't get a good education in our faith and then invariably end up only hearing about all the controversial teachings through the media. The media's job is basically to sell papers and programs and they do that very well; scandals and controversial teachings make for good headlines and the media tend to focus on them. This may be fine for making money, but it's certainly not the way to learn about your faith. I've always found that anyone I know who really has what I'd call a "living faith," doesn't have serious issues with the Church's moral teaching. This isn't because they blindly accept what makes no sense to them just because "the Church says so," but because their relationship with God is primary. Once people develop a proper relationship with God, all these other controversial issues tend to fall into place. Just about everyone struggles with some aspect of the Church's teachings. The problem is that often we're presented with all the difficult issues first, and then the Church just turns many people off. Our relationship with God has to come first.

Here is another piece of Scripture that I find very useful when it comes to Church teaching. Jesus said to the people:

> The Scribes and the Pharisees occupy the chair of Moses. You must therefore do and observe what they tell you; but do not be guided by what they do, since they do not practice what they preach. (Matthew 23:2–3)

It's interesting to note that at the time Jesus said these words, the religious authorities and people obviously had similar problems. The people passing on the teaching of God were causing scandal, because they didn't live the message they were teaching. Nonetheless, Jesus says that we should listen to what they teach, since they "occupy the chair of Moses," but that we shouldn't be guided by how they act. In other words, their teaching is what's important, even if they don't live it themselves. The exact same advice applies to us today. Even if we're scandalized by the way some priests or religious live, we must separate the behavior of some from the teaching they're passing on. What's important is that the teaching is from God, even if those who pass it on do so badly, or in a way that makes it more difficult for us to believe that teaching. Obviously, it would be a great help if the people who represent the Church were inspiring; however, even if they're not, it doesn't take away from the fact that this is God's message and not something human.

Every so often God raises up holy people to remind us of what is possible: John Paul II, Mother Teresa of Calcutta, St. Thérèse of Lisieux, saints Francis and Clare of Assisi and many others have been a huge inspiration to the world through the witness of their own lives. Frequently, God will bring about great reform in His Church through one single person. We are only instruments, and hopefully we never forget it.

PHYSICAL MIRACLES

Earlier I spoke about the many miracles that take place through confession, which are just as real as any physical miracles. That said, hundreds of physical miracles have also taken place—in Lourdes and many other places—that often go unheard of. One such miracle happened to a friend of mine's son, a boy called Joe.

I've known this family for a long time and have baptized several of Sandra and her husband's six beautiful children. It's a fairly busy house, as you can imagine. A few years ago Joe, who was three at the time, began to get severe pain below his stomach. It turned out that he had an inflamed appendix, which subsequently burst. Emergency surgery was carried out and Joe very nearly died, but thankfully he survived and is still with us today. Joe was extremely sick for several weeks and for months afterwards was very weak. Since he'd been born, Joe had also suffered from severe eczema, even though his twin sister never showed any signs of it. The poor child's skin was continually raw and bleeding, since he'd scratch it at night while asleep, if he managed to sleep at all. His eczema became so severe that he was on several courses of antibiotics at the same time, and had most of his body covered in "wet-bandages" to help his skin heal and prevent him from doing more damage. Sandra told me that it would take her an hour and twenty minutes to put the bandages on Joe in the morning and another hour and twenty minutes to take them off in the evening. A skin specialist had told them that Joe's was a very severe case, while their own family doctor had said it was one of the worst conditions he'd ever seen. Sandra and her husband decided to bring him to Lourdes to pray for him, as he'd been so sick from the surgery and the eczema. For some reason which Sandra can't explain, she took photographs of Joe's legs before they went to Lourdes.

When Our Lady appeared to St. Bernadette in 1854, she told her at one stage to dig in the earth with her hands. Bernadette unearthed a spring of water. Our Lady told Bernadette that many people would come to these waters and be healed. As time passed and the sick people who came to Lourdes grew so numerous, baths were built to enable people to dip themselves in the healing waters in a more organized way. Today people still come to these baths in great numbers.

In 2006, Joe, then aged six, and his mother arrived in Lourdes on a Monday; however, it wasn't until Thursday before they were able to go to the baths. When Joe and Sandra arrived, Joe was told that he shouldn't take off the bandages because his skin was so bad. After Joe came from the baths, he noticed that all his bandages were dry. He mentioned this to one of his uncles who was with him. They then boarded a bus as their group was going to celebrate the holy mass. In the church, Joe began saying to his mother, "Mammy, take off the bandages, I've been healed." Sandra recalls that she just dismissed this as Joe playing up, as he often did. However, Joe kept telling her that he was healed and began to say it to others there, too, including the doctor travelling with them.

Finally, he said to his mother, "Mammy, I've been healed. Why don't you believe me?" Sandra began to get suspicious and replied, "I do believe you." When they returned to the hotel, she took off Joe's bandages and found that his skin was dramatically better. When they got back to Ireland, she brought him again to the family doctor, who was amazed at how much his legs had improved. He subsequently did a full medical report on his skin, and the treatments that Joe had been on, and concluded by saying that apart from a slight dryness of the skin, the eczema was almost completely gone.

Chapter Five

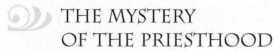 THE MYSTERY
OF THE PRIESTHOOD

BUT I AM THE WEAKEST

IN THE BOOK OF JUDGES, there's a story about a man called Gideon (see Judges, chapters 6–8). The people of Israel were being destroyed by the Midianites and were in great distress. Then one day the angel of the Lord appeared to Gideon and said: "The Lord is with you, valiant warrior!" Gideon quickly replies, "If the Lord is with us, how come we are being wiped out?" The angel then tells Gideon that God is going to rescue his people through him. But Gideon asks why God is picking him, since "My clan is the weakest in Manasseh and I am the least important of my father's family" (Judges 6:15). In other words, "Why are you picking the weakest person of the weakest family?" It doesn't make much sense, does it? But God assures him that it is God's own power that will win this victory and so Gideon needn't fear. Later on, and to further prove the point, God reduces Gideon's army from 32,000 men to three hundred men and tells Gideon the reason why He is doing this:

> There are too many people with you for me to put Mid-
> ian into their power; Israel might claim the credit for them-
> selves at my expense: they might say, "My own hand has
> rescued me." (Judges 7:2)

What is going on here? What general would pick the
weakest man to lead his troops into battle and then reduce
his numbers to almost nothing? This makes no sense from
a human point of view. The important message here is that
God wants to make it quite clear that it is *His* power that
will bring about the victory. If Gideon was already a great
leader and conquered the Midianites with a huge army, it
might not occur to people that this was God's work. However, when the least likely person is chosen and defeats a
great army with only a handful of men, then everyone says,
"It's a miracle. Look at what God has done!'

This kind of story is by no means restricted to the Old
Testament. Down through the centuries, God continues to
call what are often considered very "unsuitable" people,
by human standards at least. The reason is the same: God
wants it to be clear that it's His work that we're witnessing
and that we are only instruments. St. Francis of Assisi is a
good example. Francis was what you might call a religious
"hippy." He fell in love with God and decided to try and
live the Bible literally. He left everything behind including
his clothes, and walked away to live a life of poverty and
simplicity. Many thought he was crazy and yet through
him God brought about huge change and renewal in the
Church, which has carried on to this day. St. John Marie
Vianney—better known as the Curé of Ars—is another.
He was a simple priest, considered not much use for anything "important" and so was sent to a remote village in
southern France. The one thing that both these men had

was a passion for God. They were open to God and so God was able to do extraordinary things through them. Half of France was converted thanks to the work of St. John Vianney. Today he is the patron saint of priests. God has used thousands of men and women in the same way. All God needs is an open heart.

Perhaps one of the strangest things that Jesus did before He ascended to heaven was to entrust His Church to His priests, the first Apostles. These were ordinary, uneducated, sinful men. Down through the centuries God has continued to call similar men and ask them to fulfil a certain duty in His Church. They're the ones who bring the Eucharist to the people in the holy mass; they're the instruments of God's forgiveness in confession; they are to be Christ in the world in a unique way. In the seminary we used often joke about the fact that it always seemed to be the holiest guys who left before they were ordained. Perhaps it was true. Like Gideon, God uses people who are often weaker, rather than the stronger. What is essential is that they are open to Him.

Having worked with many priests, and being a priest myself, I can say for certain that most of the priests I know are very dedicated men, who do their best to bring God to others in whatever way they can. At the same time, most of us aren't particularly talented, aren't extraordinary speakers or leaders, and yet God is happy to go on working through us, not withstanding our weaknesses, and even in spite of the fact that we often make a mess of things. The difficult truth is that the weaker we are, the better God can work through us, because then we don't get in His way, so to speak. We're full of our own ideas and energy, but they may not be the right ideas. We think we know what to say, but it's really only God who knows exactly what needs to be said and, more importantly, when and where it needs to be said.

In his book *The Anointing,* which taught me a great deal, the American evangelist Benny Hinn tells his own extraordinary story of how God called him to be a preacher and worker of miracles. God taught Benny that the most important thing he could do was to pray to the Holy Spirit each day that his work would be "anointed," so that it would bear fruit. He had to pray specifically for the anointing of the Spirit. If the Holy Spirit didn't touch the words that Benny spoke and set fire to them in people's hearts, his work would be a waste of time. Benny would speak to hundreds and even thousands of people at a time and all sorts of extraordinary things would happen. People were continually healed and many came to believe in God through Benny's preaching.

Once Benny was conducting a service in Detroit. During the morning session the power of God was tangibly present and it was obvious that people were being touched by God all around him. "People began to weep," writes Benny.

> As I was speaking, some fell from their seats onto the floor. They just crumbled and sobbed. Their response was amazing. . . . I had never before felt the presence and the anointing of the Holy Spirit so powerfully in a service. (Hinn, p. 3)

After the morning service, Benny had arranged to meet a cousin of his whom he hadn't seen for some time. He went to her home and joined her and her husband for lunch. While he was enjoying this time with his cousin, Benny felt the Lord urging him to leave and pray in order to get ready for the evening session. But Benny resisted, feeling it would be rude to leave. When he got back to his hotel, which was forty-five minutes away, he was so tired that he just fell asleep. Later, as he arrived at the evening session, the crowd was twice as big as it had been that morning. As it had been so powerful in the morning he wondered if it would be just as amazing in the evening too, but then something happened.

> I got up to preach, but when I opened my mouth, there was nothing—only words. No presence. No overwhelming anointing of the Spirit. No power. I struggled. I didn't know what to do next. I could tell by the expression on their faces that many were wondering what was going on. The truth was: *Nothing* was going on. . . . Finally the service ended. It was a disaster! (see Hinn, pp. 5–6.)

This taught Benny a painful but valuable lesson, making him realize that the power of his work wasn't in what he could do himself, rather in what God was doing through him. The anointing of God's Holy Spirit was absolutely essential and God was teaching him the necessity of continually praying for that anointing and never taking it for granted. By ourselves, we've nothing to offer. It's only the power of God that can change hearts.

While many of us know this in theory, the reality often takes a bit longer to sink in. It doesn't matter how eloquent our sermons are, or how many people we visit, or all the groups that we have going in our parishes. What matters is that God blesses what we are doing, otherwise we're relying on the little *we* as individuals can do. We're only human, with limited understanding, energy, and wisdom. God, on the other hand, isn't limited in any way. The Lord knows exactly what work needs to be done, what will and will not be effective and when precisely it needs to be done.

God is the only one who can touch someone's heart, even though He continually works through human instruments. The sooner we realize this, the easier it makes our work, because then we realize that the "success" or fruitfulness of our work doesn't depend on what we can do, rather on what God will do through us.

Therefore, the most important thing that anyone who wants to be open to the work of God can do, is pray. Prayer is simply the expression of our relationship with God, and just like a relationship with any other person it takes many different forms. What is essential though, is that we give it time. We must keep turning up! If we aren't rooted in God, listening to Him, soaking ourselves each day in the Scriptures, we'll be reduced to what we can do ourselves.

This is a simple truth and yet it seems that each of us have to learn it the hard way. One of the most common things that priests suffer from is "burnout": mental and physical exhaustion. The reason why is we're trying to do our work through our own strength and naturally we're worn out in no time. It's happened to me twice. The first time I needed six months before I could go back into ministry and it took a full year before I fully recovered. It was a difficult but important lesson. The only thing I can pass on to people that's worth anything is what comes from God. If I'm to be an effective instrument I need to be tuned in to God, so that I'll hear what He wants me to do.

THE SPIRIT WILL
TEACH YOU EVERYTHING

I used often wonder what was meant in the Bible where it says that Paul, or Peter, or someone else, was "prompted by the Spirit," or "the Spirit told him. . . ." For example:

While Peter's mind was still on the vision, the Spirit told him, "Look! Some men have come to see you. Hurry down and do not hesitate to return with them; it was I who told them to come." (Acts 10:19–21)

There are many similar instances, especially in the Acts of the Apostles. Did they hear a voice, or see something? I never understood this until I began to experience it myself. The easiest way to explain it is to give you an example.

For the first two and a half years of my priesthood I worked as a chaplain in Merlin Park hospital in my hometown of Galway. This was a hospital of about 360 beds and I was the only chaplain, so there was no shortage of work. I'd usually get to see people no more than once, since there were so many people to see and most patients weren't there for very long anyway. I'd always pray that God would guide me to the people who really needed a priest, as my work could easily be taken up with visiting people who were just admitted, but didn't really need to see a priest.

One day, I was visiting one of the blocks of the hospital that was receiving new admissions. Merlin Park worked in conjunction with another, larger hospital in the city and new admissions would go to one or other hospital every second day. When I went to the nurses' station I'd be told who'd just been admitted, who was very sick, and so on. The nurse on duty informed me that there was a man who'd just been admitted who'd swallowed a deadly poison used by farmers to kill weeds. Even the smallest dose of it is lethal to humans and once taken the damage cannot be undone, because it burns its way through your body and nothing can stop it. This unfortunate man had taken a small amount and was now going to die a slow and painful death. Perhaps the hardest part for him was that he now had to face his family and explain to them what had happened. The best the medical people were able to do was to try and control the pain. The doctor told me that he would only last a couple of days.

As I approached the man's room I prayed that God would give me the wisdom I needed. I stood at the open door and said, "Hi, I'm the chaplain. I just wanted to say hello." The man was there with his son, who was probably in his late twenties, by his bed. I knew by the look on their faces that they weren't going to be too receptive toward me. I told the man that I'd heard what had happened, and that I was sorry.

Then, before I knew what was happening, I asked: "Do you regret it?" I just felt that I needed to be direct with this man, but these words came out of my mouth almost in spite of myself.

"Yes, I do," the man said.

As soon as he'd said those words I had a very strong sense of the Spirit saying to me, "That is a confession, so don't look for one." It was unmistakable. I asked if he'd like me to come in and talk.

"I don't want to make a confession," the farmer stated, straightaway.

"That's fine, you don't have to," I replied.

I asked the farmer's son if I could have a word with his father on my own. The son checked with his dad and then left, still obviously suspicious of me. I spoke to the man for a few moments and he told me how he had taken the poison on the spur of the moment and was sorry. After talking for a while I offered to give him the sacrament of the sick, which involves anointing a person on their forehead and hands with oil. In this sacrament of healing, the priest also gives the recipient absolution for their sins, and prays that

God will heal them and give them strength. When I offered him the sacrament he said again quite forcefully, "I don't want to make a confession." I told him he didn't have to, but just to tell God in his own mind that he was sorry for anything he'd done wrong. I gave him the sacrament of the sick, told him that I'd pray for him, and left. I never saw him again.

Several weeks later I heard through someone else that that man had refused to see two other priests in the first hospital where he was admitted before I saw him. If I'd known that, I wouldn't have gone to see him, as I'm not one to look for extra hardship! I also heard that he'd been able to make his peace with God and that he'd died greatly consoled by this. His family were also very comforted when they heard what had happened. Now that is the work of the Holy Spirit, sending me to people whom I could easily have missed or avoided, and saying what needed to be said, even unknown to myself. It's incidents like these that help me to be aware of how much I'm only an instrument. I've never forgotten it.

At the same time, there have been many times when I've felt hopelessly inadequate and unable to do anything right. However, I've prayed for the people in these situations and I believe that God always brings good out of every situation that's entrusted to Him, even if we never see the results. Perhaps, at times, it's also necessary for us to realize how little we can do. Many times I've found myself with a patient that I wouldn't normally have met on my rounds and it would be someone who really needed to talk. I've no doubt that it is the "prompting" of the Holy Spirit that guides me to these people.

One afternoon I was cycling home from town and was going to stop off in a church to celebrate mass, as I was on vacation at that time. Just as I came close to the turn for the church I had a very strong sense that I shouldn't celebrate the mass now, but that I should go home instead. By now I'd learned to listen to this kind of "instruction," although I realized it could just as easily be my imagination. So I continued home and there I found a message on my answering machine to say that a lady who'd worked with me in the hospital some years before had died and her funeral was at five o'clock at a different church. It was now four. I didn't think I'd make it, but I decided to chance it and I arrived just in time for the mass. I was so grateful to have been able to go, as this particular lady had helped a lot in the church and had been a gifted flower arranger. Her husband, whom I also knew, really appreciated that I'd come. This is more of the Spirit's work.

I've learned that the Spirit prompts us regularly if we're listening. One could be cynical and say that these things are just coincidences, but when you believe in God you begin to realize that He's far more involved in our lives than we usually think. The problem is that most of the time we're not listening. Again, this is why prayer is an essential aspect of the life of anyone who wants to seriously follow Jesus.

ALTER CHRISTUS

The priest is called *alter Christus* in Latin, which means "another Christ." Since I'm only a human being, this can be difficult to grasp. I'm only too aware of my own weaknesses. In spite of this, it's through ministering to other people whom I continually meet that I've come to see just how true this is. I'm often amazed at how people who've never met me before will tell me the most intimate things about their life and ask me to pray for them. Some will tell me about spiritual experiences they've had and others will be curious just to talk to me. This isn't because I'm an extraordinary human being, rather because somehow they see Jesus in the priest. A priest is supposed to be a man of God, someone who reminds people of God, a person who lives completely for God. It's also for this reason that scandals caused by a priest are so serious. They haven't only betrayed a human trust, but somehow a much deeper one, too, and this causes great pain. Yet in spite of our many weaknesses, God is still prepared to go on working through us. Indeed, perhaps it's because we are so weak that God uses us.

The Bible is full of examples of how people resisted God's call because they felt they weren't up to the task. When God called Moses and told him that he was to go to Pharaoh and demand the release of his people, Moses protested vehemently that he wasn't the man for the job:

> But Moses said to the Lord, "O my Lord, I have never been eloquent, neither in the past nor even now that you have spoken to your servant; but I am slow of speech and slow of tongue." Then the Lord said to him, "Who gives speech to mortals? Who makes them mute or deaf, seeing or blind? Is it not I, the Lord? Now go and I will be with your mouth and teach you what you are to speak." But he said, "O my Lord, please send someone else." (Exodus 4:10–13)

Moses wasn't the only one either. Nearly all the prophets had the same reaction. Jeremiah also objected, saying that he wasn't able to speak for God:

> Now the word of the Lord came to me saying, "Before I formed you in the womb, I knew you, and before you were

born I consecrated you; I appointed you a prophet to the nations."

Then I said, "Ah, Lord God! Truly I do not know how to speak, for I am only a boy." But the Lord said to me, "Do not say, 'I am only a boy'; for you shall go to all to whom I send you, and you shall speak whatever I command you." (Jeremiah 1:4–7)

When the Lord called the prophet Jonah to go and speak to the people of Nineveh (see Jonah chapter 1), he took off in the opposite direction and boarded a ship to try to escape. But after the storm almost wrecked their ship, Jonah was thrown overboard only to be swallowed by a great fish. Having escaped from the fish, God calls him again. The second time Jonah obeys, realizing there is no escape.

One of the most humorous passages in the Bible to my mind is where God calls Ananias to go and lay hands on Saul (later called Paul), who's just seen a vision of Jesus on his way to Damascus. Ananias tries to explain to God that this may not be such a wise choice (basically telling God, "Do you realize who this guy is?!"):

Now there was a disciple in Damascus named Ananias. The Lord said to him in a vision, "Ananias." He answered, "Here I am, Lord." The Lord said to him, "Get up and go to the street called Straight, and at the house of Judas look for a man of Tarsus named Saul. At this moment he is praying, and he has seen in a vision a man named Ananias come in and lay his hands on him so that he might regain his sight." But Ananias answered, "Lord, I have heard from many about this man, how much evil he has done to your saints, in Jerusalem; and here he has authority from the chief priests to bind all who invoke your name." But the

Lord said to him, "Go, for he is an instrument whom I have chosen to bring my name before Gentiles and kings and before the people of Israel." (Acts 9:10–15)

One thing for certain is that we most certainly don't understand why God chooses the people He does. It's very likely that we'd pick completely different people who are more "suitable" for the job. And yet what it comes down to isn't our ability to do anything, but the fact that God wants to use us. We cannot explain this and I can safely say I know of many priests who often question whether it was such a good idea for God to call them. Naturally, we tend to judge things by human standards, but God doesn't work in a way that makes any sense to us and indeed often does so in a way that baffles us.

Priests are ordinary and often weak people, yet God has asked us to serve Him in this particular role. I don't understand this, but I certainly believe it. I was recently at a reunion for priests ordained from Maynooth seminary. It was amazing so see men there who were celebrating anywhere from one year up to sixty-five years of priesthood. There were probably not that many geniuses or extraordinary people among us, and yet for some reason God called us to serve Him.

CELIBACY

Perhaps more than ever, people find it very hard today to understand why priests aren't allowed to marry. It's often argued that if priests were allowed to marry it would sort out many of the problems in the Church. I disagree. One of the difficulties here is that in the West especially, we're repeatedly told that we must be sexually active or we won't be fulfilled. Our society has become obsessed with sex. Generally anything to do with celibacy is only presented to people negatively. It's understood to mean that you can *not* be married, as opposed to seeing it as a way of dedicating your life completely to God, which people have been doing for centuries.

We are told that if priests could marry it would help resolve the shortage of priests. In the Eastern Rite Church, which is also Catholic, the priests are married and yet they have the very same problems that we have. We're also given the impression that celibacy is a cause of child sexual abuse. I've had it said to my face, "Well, at least if you could get married we wouldn't have any more child abuse." That is naïve. Pedophilia has done untold damage in the Church, but the truth is that it has nothing to do with celibacy. The highest percentage of child abuse actually happens in the family home. Pedophilia is a sickness in itself and a very serious problem that we must do everything possible to overcome, but not being married has nothing to do with it.

Priests are called to be celibate because we believe it to be a personal invitation from God to dedicate ourselves completely to Him, to imitate the life of Jesus, and also so that we can serve others in a way that wouldn't be possible if we were married. We freely choose to do this. Before I was ordained a deacon with my classmates, we were all required to make promises. First of all, we had to recite the Apostles Creed and then we stated publicly that we had come freely of our own doing and without any compulsion. We were freely choosing to renounce marriage because we wanted to dedicate our lives to God in this way. We gave up the possibility of marriage not because it was bad, but because we were willing to make this sacrifice for the sake of following Jesus Christ. This is certainly not something everyone understands or can accept. I'm not sure that I understand it myself at times, but I most certainly believe in it. Would I like to be married? Of course: It's one of the most natural desires in the world. But that doesn't mean I think that celibacy should be abolished. Do I struggle with celibacy? Certainly, and hardly a day goes by where I don't wonder what it would be like to be married. Yet many married people struggle with being married, too.

Some priests find that they're not suited to a life of celibacy and leave. I always feel sad for them, because it must be very traumatic to have to leave the priesthood, and yet I've no doubt that God understands them and will use them in a different way. My uncle, Fr. Kevin Kennedy, who died in August 2004, said of celibacy: "Certainly it can be lonely, but the spiritual consolations are enormous." From what I've experienced over the last ten years as a priest, that is quite accurate. When people question me as to why I took on celibacy and didn't want to be married, I answer: "Of course I'd like to have been married, but the call of God to be a priest was stronger."

Each day, I must choose again to live a celibate life for God. This means that, each day, I must ask God for His help. Mostly it isn't a problem, but some days it can be extremely difficult. The biggest mistake that I could make would be to think that I could live this way of life by my own strength. I couldn't and cannot, but then God does not expect me to. God expects me to rely on His help (what we call "grace") which He freely and generously gives to all who ask. This is also the idea of the sacraments of marriage and holy orders (priesthood). In these sacraments, we ask God for His help and blessing to enable us to live this way of life. God takes this seriously and we should too, turning and asking Him for help as often as is necessary.

A priest is supposed to be loving to the people he ministers to, while at the same time not getting too involved with any one person. This may sound easy, but in practice it can be quite tricky. People who are vulnerable will often cling to someone who offers support and so it's wise to try and keep a certain distance. That isn't always so easy to achieve. To attain this balance, it's essential for a priest to be someone who continually turns to prayer and tries to live a balanced lifestyle, with the support of friends and colleagues to help him stay healthy. Thankfully, I've been blessed with great friends without whom I'm quite sure I wouldn't have survived as a priest.

Chapter Six

 THE EUCHARIST

THE GREATEST PRIVILEGE for any priest is to be able to celebrate the Eucharist, or "the Holy Sacrifice of the Mass," as it's also called. The Eucharist is the center of our faith—the source of our life—because it is Jesus himself hidden in the form of bread and wine. To be God's instrument so that Christ becomes present on the altar is a mind-blowing idea. Indeed, I often think that if I gave it much consideration, I simply wouldn't be able to celebrate mass at all, because it is too frightening. The Son of God, through whom everything was created, becomes present in the priest's hands on the altar. How can it be that God allows Himself to be handled by me, or any other priest in this way? I don't understand it, but I believe it. I know that the transformation isn't just a symbol, or merely some kind of holy bread, because I've seen the effects it has on people for one thing.

In the hospital where I worked I'd bring Holy Communion to people each day. I noticed that it nearly always caused a reaction of one kind or another. One time, it happened that a man just started crying when I brought the Eucharist into his room. He'd been through a lot and the

presence of Christ had a profound effect on him. Sometimes it caused a reaction of anger or rebellion in people.
People were seldom neutral, however; they seemed to know
that something special was happening when the Eucharist
was brought around. No ordinary bread could have this
effect on people, but the Eucharist isn't ordinary bread.
Under the simple appearance of bread and wine, Christ
becomes present to us. The Son of God makes Himself
available to us, putting himself at our disposal even when
we're not respectful.

One thing I found particularly difficult in Merlin Park
was the indifference or disrespect that I met at times. Sometimes people received Holy Communion and immediately
went back to reading the paper, as though I'd given them a
piece of gum. I'd usually suggest that they pray for a minute, but it was never easy. One day, on an especially bad day,
as I walked the corridor I found myself praying, "Lord, it
isn't right that they treat you like this!" I then had a sense
of the Lord saying to me, "Murchadh, I'm so keen to come
to each person that I'm prepared to put up with a lot of disrespect." I was surprised at this thought and it changed my
attitude somewhat, but I never found it easy. Nonetheless, I
regularly have to remind myself that Jesus left his disciples
under no illusions about being popular and, indeed, that
they'd be persecuted simply because they were associated
with him:

> If the world hates you, you must realize that it hated me
> before it hated you. . . .
> If they persecuted me, they will persecute you too; if they
> kept my word, they will keep your as well. (John 15:18,
> 20b)

Fr. Des O'Malley once told me that he had to meet a woman in a hotel lobby who was practicing witchcraft. As soon as he approached her she said to him, "There's something in your pocket that I don't like." He was carrying the Eucharist with him at the time. She refused to talk to him until he put it in the car. She could sense the presence of the Eucharist straightaway.

THE HIDDEN CHRIST

What is it that keeps drawing people back to the mass, in spite of the many excuses they have not to come? So often people complain of boring liturgies, bad preaching, poor music, etc., and yet they keep returning. What else could it be but the presence of Christ in the Eucharist? It is a strange thought that in every church around the world, where the holy mass is celebrated by a priest, Jesus becomes present on the altar in the form of bread and wine. Whether it's in some of the breathtaking basilicas of the world, like St. Peter's in Rome, or in a simple little church with just a handful of people attending, Christ is just as present in each one.

So why does Jesus not make his presence more obvious to everyone? Imagine if once in a while people could physically see that it was Jesus, or if blinding light came from the tabernacle when we opened it. Wouldn't this be a great help to our faith? Perhaps it would, but it seems that God prefers to have us believe without this kind of consolation or help. It would be a lot easier to believe if we could see a tangible sign that left us in no doubt about what is before us, but then it would be a different kind of faith. In remaining hidden, Jesus draws us to a deeper belief. We cannot see, but we believe, because it is Jesus who has told us this truth.

In St. John's Gospel, after Jesus has worked the miracle of multiplying the bread and feeding the thousands, he then speaks these extraordinary words:

> I am the bread of life. No one who comes to me will ever hunger. . . . If you do not eat the flesh of the son of man and drink his blood, you cannot have life within you. (John 6:35, 53)

Was this just a way of speaking, or an exaggeration to make a point? No, Jesus meant what he said and these words are repeated four times in the Gospel (6:35, 48, 51, 53). It's one of the teachings that caused the most resistance and John tells us that after Jesus gave this teaching many of his disciples stopped following him (see John 6:66). It was simply too much, they couldn't take it in. But the interesting thing is Jesus' own reaction when people started to walk away from him. He doesn't run after them and say, "Wait, let me explain what I really mean." Instead he turns to the Apostles and says, "What about you? Do you want to go away, too?" (John 6:67). He doesn't change anything he said, or try to convince anyone to understand what he meant. This was his teaching and he meant every word of it. Then at the last supper, Jesus celebrates the first mass:

> Now as they were eating, Jesus took bread, and when he had said the blessing he broke it and gave it to the disciples. "Take it and eat," he said, "this is my body." Then he took a cup, and when he had given thanks he handed it to them saying, "Drink from this, all of you, for this is my blood, the blood of the covenant, poured out for many for the forgiveness of sins. (Matthew 26:26–28)

Jesus makes himself present in the bread and wine. He asks his disciples to eat the bread and drink from the cup and also to repeat this ritual in his memory. This is what we continue to do to this day.

The fact that the meal was the celebration of the Passover meal is also important. The Passover was the feast that the Jewish people celebrated to mark the night they were freed from slavery in Egypt (see Exodus 12). Their time in Egypt also symbolically represents slavery to sin. That night the angel of death was to pass through the land of Egypt and strike down all the firstborn of the Egyptians. It was to be the last and most terrible plague that God would inflict on Pharaoh, so that he'd know that the God of Israel was to be listened to. Pharaoh would then drive the people out of Egypt. During the meal the people were told to sacrifice a lamb (or kid goat) and to put its blood on the doorposts of the house as a sign that these people belonged to God. The angel of death would recognize the blood of the lamb and pass over the house (hence the name "pass-over"). So, symbolically, the people were saved by the blood of the lamb. They were also told to be dressed for the road while they ate the meal. They were to eat unleavened bread with bitter herbs, which symbolized their hurried departure. As they had to leave quickly they didn't have time to allow the bread to rise: hence the use of unleavened bread. (The bread that is used in the mass today is also unleavened.)

At his last supper, as Jesus celebrated the Passover meal with the Apostles, he told them that this (unleavened) bread was now his body, which was to be given up for all people. At the end of the meal he announced that the cup of wine was the cup of his blood—the blood that would seal the new and eternal covenant with God, to win eternal life for his people. Jesus was the new "lamb" to be sacrificed to save the people. Remember the words of John the Baptist when he saw Jesus? "Look! There is the lamb of God who takes away the sins of the world" (John 1:29). This is why the mass is a re-presentation of the sacrifice of Jesus on Calvary, which is also related to God freeing his people from Egypt (the slavery of sin), celebrated each year with the Passover meal. Why did Jesus do this strange thing? No doubt there are many reasons, but I'm sure that it was above all because he desired to remain with us and be available to us in a profound way.

When someone we love dies we often say that they're still with us in spirit. Many people keep items belonging to their loved ones, by which to remember them and feel close to them. But Jesus did much more than give us a symbolic reminder of himself. He promised that he'd remain with us always and offered us this extraordinary gift of his body and blood so we can experience his presence with us, even every day if we wish. This is the most important reason why Jesus left us with the Eucharist, simply so he could remain close to us.

From the first time Jesus gave this teaching about his body and blood it has continually caused controversy. Sometimes the early Christians were suspected of cannibalism, and you can see why: Talk of eating human flesh and blood is definitely strange. Yet who could come up with such a bizarre teaching and get away with it except God? It's hard to believe any human being would concoct such an idea and really expect people to believe it, to say nothing of it becoming an accepted teaching for millions all over the world. Each day when a priest celebrates the holy mass, Jesus Christ, the Son of God, the eternal Word made flesh,[7] becomes present in the bread and wine that he holds in his hands. This happens because the Holy Spirit works through the priest, and not because the latter has some kind of special power as a human being.

IT WASN'T MY IDEA

In the earliest account of the mass, St. Paul says:

For the tradition I received from the Lord and also handed on to you, is that on the night he was betrayed, the Lord Jesus took some bread, and after he had given thanks, he broke it and he said, "This is my body, which is for you; do this in remembrance of me." (1 Corinthians 11:23–24)

What is worth noting here is the first line: "For the tradition I received from the Lord and also handed on to you. . . ." Paul is clearly stating that this idea didn't come from him, or indeed from any other human source, but from the Lord Jesus himself. This is why the mass is the most important prayer that we have, because it was the Lord who gave it to us and also commanded us to repeat it.

What happens in each mass is also quite astonishing. First of all, we listen to the word of God in the Scriptures, as people have been doing for about 2,500 years. We constantly seek God's guidance and wisdom and He continually offers it to us through His word, which is why we never replace the Scriptures with any other kind of "better" or more "interesting" literature. Other writings may be more creatively put together, or easier on the ear, but they aren't the word of God. It has a life all of its own and its effect on people is astounding. In the letter to the Hebrews God's word is described as "something alive and active":

It cuts more incisively than any two-edged sword: it can seek out the place where soul is divided from spirit, or joints from marrow: it can pass judgement on secret emotions and thoughts. (Hebrews 4:12–13, see also Revelations 1:16; 2:12; and Ephesians 6:17)

SO THAT SINS MAY BE FORGIVEN

As well as listening to the word of God in the Scriptures, where God speaks to us and guides us through His word, we're also present to the greatest miracle on earth, where God the Son is offered to God the Father for the forgiveness of sins. We become present to the event on Calvary where God made it possible for us to have eternal life with Him when we die. This happens in each mass. As the priest says the words of consecration—"This is my body . . . this is the cup of my blood"—we are present at the event of Jesus' death on the cross.

It isn't that this event happens again and again, rather that we become present to it. It only needed to be done once, since it was the only completely perfect sacrifice. The Son of God took the sins of humanity on Himself and suffered God's punishment for them, so that He could win forgiveness on our behalf. That forgiveness is now offered as a gift to anyone who wants it. It is profound, yet simple. In the letter to the Romans, St. Paul puts it like this:

Since all have sinned and fall short of the glory of God, they are redeemed by His grace as a gift . . . to be received through faith. (Romans 3:23)

We don't have to do anything but accept what has been done for us, through faith. I take great consolation from this line of Scripture. As a priest I regularly hear people worrying about whether God will forgive them or not, as they become aware of their own sinfulness; and the more spiritual they become, the more they recognize this. In fact, we will *never* be good enough for God by our own doing. At the same time, our inadequacy doesn't matter since it has been taken care of for us by Jesus, who has done for us what we couldn't do for ourselves. All we have to do is accept it as a free gift. The strange thing is that this act is almost too simple for most of us and we continue to strive to become holy or good enough for God, something we'll never achieve. We should, of course, strive to be better, and God knows most people do, but it's essential that we remember that ultimately we can only surrender to God and say "Thank you." Everything is a gift.

Each time I celebrate the holy mass, the phrase that strikes me again and again is the line at the end of the consecration, where the priest prays over the chalice and says the words, "so that sins may be forgiven." In essence, this is what each mass is about. The whole purpose of the life, death and resurrection of Christ is so that sins can be forgiven. If we find ourselves wondering whether or not we'll make it to heaven, we should remember this line. God created us to share in His happiness and God will bring us to that happiness unless we consciously and deliberately reject Him.

THE FIRST SIN

Back at the beginnings of the human race, our first parents rebelled against God. We don't know exactly what happened, only that something occurred that caused us to lose the original harmony that God had given to us. The story of Adam and Eve in the book of Genesis is a clever piece of writing that tries to elucidate what occurred (see Genesis, chapters 2 and 3), but the account isn't meant to be taken literally. Rather it's a way of explaining some profound truths about the human condition. In pointing out the trees the humans weren't to eat from, God was saying that we were limited as human beings and that we should recognize and respect those limits. We weren't to be the ones who could decide what was ultimately good and evil. That was God's department. If we started playing God ourselves, we'd be in trouble and out of our depth.

The story relates that through temptation our first parents gave in to the idea that they didn't need to heed God's word. God warned Adam and Eve to respect the limits He'd given them, but they rejected his word and chose to listen to another voice. They thought they knew better. Having rejected God's word, Adam and Eve began to feel shame, guilt, and fear—some of the consequences of sin. They'd never experienced these emotions before and didn't understand what was happening to them. So God in His goodness confronted them and helped them understand what was wrong. This wasn't so much God chastizing the first sinners, as helping them to see what had happened. God is always merciful. One of the results of "the Fall"[8] was that we then felt isolated from God and from each other. We became suspicious of God. Could we really be sure that God was good? This is something that you still hear all the time today. When evil happens in the world we're quick to blame God; we're much slower to recognize that the fault is probably our own. For example, people ask "How can God allow so many people to starve in the world?" The truth is that there is more than enough food to go around, but it's because of human greed that there is such an imbalance.

The most serious consequence of the Fall was that we lost the possibility of eternal life with God, which God had created for us. How could we possibly win this back? How could any human being offer something to God in atonement for the sin of the human race, since everything we have comes from God in the first place? For any appropriate offering to be made to God, it would have to come from a human being, since the sin was a human one. But the only one who could offer God anything worthwhile would have to be divine. This is why the Son of God took on human nature: "The Word became flesh and lived among us" (John 1:14). By offering his life and death on our behalf, Jesus made the perfect atonement for our sin, since he was both fully human and fully divine. No one else could have done this. Every time we offer the holy mass we re-present (make present again) this offering of God the Son to God the Father—and this is one sacrifice that cannot be refused. That is why the mass is so powerful and is offered for everything and everyone we can think of.

When people say they find mass boring, it's an indication that they don't understand what is going on. You will seldom hear someone say they're bored at a funeral—because they know why they're there. If we understand what the mass is about, the question of it being boring doesn't arise.

THE HOLINESS OF THE PRIEST

Sometimes I hear people saying that they'd love to get such-and-such a priest to offer mass for them, because he's "holy." What this means is they're drawn to one individual because he gives them a sense of being close to God. There's nothing wrong with this, of course, but it would be a mistake to think that the power of the mass depends on how holy the priest is. If the priest is a terrible sinner and doesn't live as he should, it certainly won't help people's faith, but it doesn't mean for a second that Jesus is any less present in the Eucharist, or that the mass is any less powerful. Likewise, if the priest is very holy, it's a great help for others to see, but it doesn't mean that the mass is more powerful. God uses the priest as an instrument regardless of how holy or otherwise he is.

Obviously we priests should have lives that inspire others, but this is all-too-often not the case. Either way, God is equally present in the mass, in confession, and in all the sacraments, regardless of the priest's attitude: God would never let the power of His presence depend on the holiness of the priest. This is worth remembering, especially at times when scandals caused by priests occur. Terrible though the scandals may be, God doesn't rely on the priest being "good enough" for him to be present.

Chapter Seven

THE DAY THE BUBBLE BURST

HOSPITAL

WHEN I WAS A DEACON, I was sent to a hospital for a course called Clinical Pastoral Education (CPE) that was designed to help people in ministry. It provided excellent training in the skills that can help any kind of ministry, and focused on communication and listening skills. However, I found that, just as with any kind of work, it was almost like starting afresh when I began to work in "the field," as it were.

As you've already seen, hospital ministry, while often deeply rewarding, can be very intense. Dealing with sickness and death all day long can be exhausting. Of course, it's very satisfying when people appreciate your work as a priest, and they're probably more open to you than they'd normally be. However, not everyone understands what you're doing and you can encounter a lot of misunderstanding. At the Christmas party one year, a doctor from another hospital said to me, "Don't you find it difficult working among all these 'professional' people?" He obviously didn't see the role of a priest as being very serious.

I explained to him that it really was a matter of faith: If you believed what I believed, then the role of the priest was essential; if you didn't, then the priest was irrelevant. On the other hand, a patient who was a retired doctor said to me: "Do you realize that you're the most important person in the hospital?" It was kind of him to say so.

One of the practical difficulties I had to face was that I looked ten years younger than my age. Most of our family are the same. As a result, people sometimes wouldn't take me seriously, at least initially. One lady who was in for a hip replacement, told me, "When I saw you walking past and how young you were, I said to myself, 'His blessings will be no good,' so I called my own priest in instead." How disarming! Another lady I came to visit had her back to me and was talking to a friend, who indicated that she had a visitor. I introduced myself the usual way—"Hello, I'm the chaplain." Before I could say another word she looked over her shoulder at me and said, "Sure, you're too young to know anything about anything!"

Working with the sick and dying is a great privilege—a wonderful grounding in the reality of life. People die in the hospital every day, largely because many of them are brought in who are already close to death. Coping with so much death sharpens your sense of what life is about. I also found it interesting to see how people came to the hospital full of their own self-importance, but usually after a short time realized that they had to wait to be attended to, just like everyone else. In this way, sickness brings people down to the same level. I also found it gratifying—though not surprising—to see how elderly people were usually the most patient and kind. Their experience of life had mellowed them and they were generally quite tolerant. Young people were often the most demanding.

I came across some extraordinary stories in the hospital, too. I met an old man who lived in a remote part of the countryside. He was a farmer and he had been out burning gorse. (Gorse or furze is a prickly bush that grows very fast and is usually considered a weed.) While he was setting fire to the gorse, his coat had become entangled in barbed wire and he was engulfed in the flames. His dog took off and ran a great distance to alert a neighbor, guiding the latter back to the old man. The dog had saved his life, although the man was badly burned.

The work in the hospital seemed endless and unrelenting. Unknown to myself, I was pushing myself too hard and had been for some years. Eventually, this started to take its toll. I began to find it more difficult to cope and to dread the pager going off. I was on-call five and a half days a week, twenty-four hours a day. This was really a spillover from former days when there'd been two chaplains (and half the turn-over of patients). It was an unhealthy set up, but when you have just started off in ministry you're not always wise enough to see these things. Consequently, I became more and more exhausted and started falling ill.

Of course, I couldn't see this myself and kept saying to friends of mine who were concerned for me, "I'm just having a few busy days." But the "busy days" became more frequent, with less space between them. Finally, my body began to say "enough" and I started to get very sick. It came to a head one weekend in November. I realized that I badly needed a break and right away. I went to an older priest in the diocese and explained how stressed I was and that I felt I shouldn't remain in the hospital after that year. He could see that I was a wreck and advised me to take a break. I managed to get a few days off that week and headed up to Dublin on a Tuesday for the opening of an art exhibition. My sister Éadaín was the artist. I traveled by car with a friend of mine called Ian, with whom I'd been friends since 1989. He was very much a soulmate as well as a friend.

On the way to Dublin we had a long conversation about what was happening to both of us, since he was also going through a very difficult time in his life. "You need to get out of that hospital," he told me, and I knew he was right. The problem was how to do it. He said that I needed to go to the bishop and tell him that I had to take a break. While I knew he was right, I wasn't enthusiastic at the thought of having to go to the bishop and tell him that I needed to leave immediately. The next few days in Dublin were even more stressful as I went through all the possibilities of what I was going to do when I returned to Galway.

On the drive home that Thursday I knew I needed to get to a doctor, see a psychologist friend of mine, and go to the bishop—in that order. I prayed that God would make it all happen and of course in his goodness God opened all the doors and I managed to see all three people in the one day and in the right order. The doctor (also a friend of mine) gave me the onceover and told me that I was suffering from emotional and physical exhaustion (also known as "burnout"). Indeed, that while I was sitting calmly in his office, I actually had a heart rate of 116! This confirmed that I wasn't imagining my condition and gave me the professional back-up that I needed. I then went to the psychologist, who was also very compassionate and wise, and she advised me to tell the bishop that I was sick, and needed time off and a place to stay. "Don't back down on any of them," she added. That was what I needed to hear.

It may sound strange that going to the bishop with this problem was such a big issue, but as a young priest it isn't what you expect to have to do after two and a half years in ministry. I was afraid that he wouldn't believe me, or that he'd dismiss it as an overreaction. In fairness to the bishop, he was very understanding and acted straight away. I was given the time off I needed and a place to stay. I was very grateful to the bishop for his kindness and for looking after me as well as he did, but I'm ultimately sure I'd never would have had the guts to leave without Ian's encouragement.

The next four months were a time of great darkness. It was deeply humiliating to have to leave the hospital so suddenly. I'd no idea how exhausted I was myself and this only became apparent when I stopped. I fell into a depression. What was perhaps most frightening for me was that I wasn't even sure what was happening; I'd never experienced anything like it before. Friends kept asking me what was wrong and the difficulty was that I couldn't even tell them, since I wasn't sure. During this time I was fortunate enough to be directed to some expert help. The psychologist I went to—a religious sister—provided me with wonderful support and direction and helped me to see that I'd been driving myself much too hard for much too long and that this burnout was in some sense inevitable because of the way I was living. She also helped me to see that it was good to get out of the hospital when I did. If I'd tried to sit it out much longer I could have become far more unwell. Apparently, it can take anything from six months to two years to recover from burnout. It was to be almost a year before I'd take up proper work again.

Depression is very difficult to explain to someone who's never experienced it. Almost everyone gets depressed to some degree, but not everyone suffers from depression. The two are often confused. When you're depressed even the simplest decisions can become virtually impossible to make. You want to meet people, but you don't want to see them; you want to do something, but you don't feel able to. Terrible disillusionment with everything can descend like a cloud. What is probably most frightening is the fear that this darkness will never go away. "What if I am left in this darkness?" you think to yourself. "How will I cope? Will I ever be able to work as a priest again?" Others will do their best to assure you that everything will be all right, but it feels impossible to believe them. I remember standing in the kitchen one day unable to decide what to eat for my lunch. I simply couldn't choose between two options. Suddenly, I realized what I was doing and forced myself to make a decision. This gives you an idea of how simple everyday steps can turn into monumental decisions when you're depressed.

Although this was a very painful time in my life, it was also a time of great growth—something I'd only see afterward. I learned a lot about myself, my limits and weaknesses. In some ways, it was one of the most helpful experiences that ever happened to me. To learn just how weak you are may not seem beneficial, but from a spiritual point of view it is one of the most profound lessons that anyone could learn. As we've seen in the story of Gideon, Jonah, Moses, and the prophets, God works powerfully through human weakness. When we're full of our own abilities and strengths, there isn't much room for God to operate; but when we're given a clear picture of how weak we are, then God can really start to work. St. Paul speaks about this several times. In spite of the fact that he'd had an amazing conversion experience, where the Lord Jesus appeared and spoke directly to him (see Acts 9:1–19) and then went on to preach the Gospel all over the Middle East, Paul also struggled greatly with his own weaknesses. He was a very clever man, well educated and with unstoppable energy, and yet notice how he writes about his own struggles:

> Therefore, to keep me from being too elated, a thorn was given me in the flesh, a messenger of Satan to torment me, to keep me from being too elated. Three times I appealed to the Lord about this, that it would leave me, but he said to me, "My grace is sufficient for you, for power is made perfect in weakness." (2 Corinthians 12:7–9)

Paul does not say what exactly this "weakness" was. Perhaps it was some kind of addiction: we'll never know. However, Paul came to realize that this was something that the Lord allowed him to suffer for his own good. It is one of those paradoxes of the spiritual life that we're more inclined to think that if we were without our various weaknesses we'd be able to serve God much better; yet it seems that the opposite is true. God will sometimes make it clear to us just how weak we are. Then we're even more conscious that it is God who is doing the work through us.

In another passage, we can hear Paul's exasperation as he finds it hard to accept his own actions:

> I do not understand my own actions. For I do not do what I want, but I do the very thing I hate. . . . I can will what is right, but I cannot do it. For I do not do the good I want, but the evil I do not want is what I do. . . . Wretched man that I am! Who will rescue me from this body of death? Thanks be to God through Jesus Christ our Lord! (Romans 7:15, 19, 24–25)

I find it comforting that someone like St. Paul, through whom God accomplished such extraordinary achievements and brought so many people to faith, could struggle in this way. It reminds me that God doesn't need the "great," but those who are open to Him and willing to be used as an instrument. It seems that often the weaker we are, the more effective we can be as God's instrument. This is a way of thinking we find difficult to get our heads around.

When we're in pain, we'll often turn to just about anything to deaden it. This is where a lot of addictions come from. One way to understand addiction is to see it as a kind of coping mechanism to kill the pain. Addiction is more a symptom than a disease, but it gets out of control and can take over our lives. In order to recover from addictive behavior, it isn't simply a question of giving up the particular addiction, but tackling the underlying problem. This is where the Twelve Step program of Alcoholics Anonymous (and all the other Twelve-Step programs) are so effective—because they provide the support network that people need and tackle the fundamental predicament of emotional dysfunction. At the deepest level, we all need emotional healing.

During this time, I also began to realize that I had an addictive personality. This, too, caused me great distress. However, once again, this recognition was also to be the source of substantial growth and healing. Thankfully, through a support group I also began to meet others who struggled in a similar way, and this was an enormous help. I was inspired by the honesty of those who shared their own struggles, and listened to the pain of others and how they coped with it. While none of those I met deliberately wanted to suffer as they were, most of them expressed gratitude at what their struggle had brought about in their life. They had come to a much deeper level of living, and discovered great joy in many of the simpler things in their life that previously they'd taken for granted.

At one stage, I began to wonder whether or not I'd be able to recover properly as long as I remained working as a priest. One evening, I had a strange experience. As I was thinking about what I'd have to do to recover, I felt the Lord saying to me: "Murchadh, in order to recover properly, would you even leave the priesthood if I asked you to?" I was shocked at this thought and began to feel that this was an unfair question even to ask. I found myself thinking, "Lord, how can you even ask this question, since I've given my life to you as a priest?"

But again I felt the Lord saying to me, "If you really want to do my will, would you be willing to leave the priesthood, if I asked you to?" My head was spinning with this idea. How could I leave the priesthood, since I felt that it was what God had called me to do and indeed what I wanted to do as well? How could I face my family and friends? And yet if I said that I wanted to do God's will in everything—well either I meant it or I didn't. With a heavy heart I said, "Yes, Lord, I will even leave the priesthood if you ask me to." Very soon afterward God made it clear to me that I wouldn't have to leave; however, I believe He put me through this "test" to purify my motivations. It's easy to say that we'll do God's will, but often we have a very fixed idea as to what "doing God's will" involves. When the path takes a sudden and dramatic change of direction, it may not seem like God's will at all, and this can be a real challenge of faith.

I'll never forget this experience as long as I live; it reminded me of the test of Abraham in chapter 22 of the book of Genesis. God asks Abraham if he'd be willir sacrifice his only son—the son through whom Go promised his descendants. Abraham trusted God and was willing to take even this extreme action to be obedient to God. However, at the last moment the angel of the Lord stops him:

> "Do not raise your hand against the boy," the angel said. "Do not harm him, for now I know you fear God. You have not refused me your own beloved son." (Genesis 22:12)

I've often heard people say that they find this story quite horrific—the idea that a man would be prepared to sacrifice his son. But the story is *meant* to be horrific; that is the point. Sometimes God can ask us to do things that seem to make little or no sense. The journey of faith is a strange one.

Around the same time I had a related occurrence. It seemed that God allowed me to experience the sinfulness of my soul as it appeared before Him. I've since spoken to several other people who've had the same experience. This only lasted for a few seconds, but it was so overwhelming that I thought it would kill me. It isn't something that I can easily put into words, as no words can adequately describe what it was like. All I can say is that it was very frightening, and if God hadn't simultaneously allowed me to understand that it was purely through His grace that I could exist at all, I would have despaired. This may not make a lot of sense, but I believe it was a great gift. It gave me a strong sense of my complete nothingness apart from God—that God brought me into existence and, in spite of my sinfulness, keeps me alive. Not only that, but God also offers me a share in His divine life, not through any merit on my part, but because of all that He's done through the death and resurrection of Jesus. God offers each one of us eternal life with Him. This incredible gift, which none of us deserve, God offers us freely and generously.

People often worry about whether or not they'll be good enough to go to heaven when they die. The truth is that none of us could ever possibly be good enough to experience life with God in heaven, but it doesn't depend on our being good enough. God makes it possible; God has created us to enjoy eternal life with Him in heaven and we will experience that happiness when we die, unless we consciously and deliberately reject it. Sadly, some people do seem to reject God by the way they live, but God's plan for us is to be with Him in heaven after this life. Therefore, if we're open to this gift, it's ours for the taking. It will happen, because God will make it happen unless we stop Him.

PROVIDENCE AND OUR LADY'S CHOICE

The human difficulty of trying to do God's will is illustrated beautifully in the life of Mary of Nazareth, the mother of Jesus. Our Lady was undoubtedly a very holy woman. She wanted to serve God with her whole life and it seems she didn't intend to have children. When the angel Gabriel appeared to her (see Luke 1:26–38) and announced that she was going to have a child, she questioned him as to how this could be. Now why would Mary question the angel when she was already in the process of getting married to Joseph? It would have been the most natural thing in the world for her to have a child as soon as they were fully married. Yet she asks the angel how this can come about since "I do not know man"? The angel replies: "The Holy Spirit will come upon you, and the power of the Most High will cover you with its shadow. And so the child will be holy and will be called Son of God" (Luke 1:35). The phrase "*and so* the child will be holy" indicates that this was to be an act of God, not a human one.

In modern English, one might put the angel's proposal like this: "Mary, God is asking you to completely put aside your own plans for your life and accept His. Are you willing to do this?" No doubt Mary had very good and holy plans for how she'd serve God with her life, but God asked her to lay them aside and follow quite unexpected ones, instead. Does this sound familiar? Many of us who try to follow God's path often find that it takes a course completely different from what we anticipated. We may feel as though everything has failed, or even that we've let God down. However, it's important to remember that, as long as we're open to doing God's will and do our best to accept what happens, we're being faithful to God. If we honestly offer to serve God in our lives, then God will take that offer seriously, perhaps even more seriously than we expected!

The difficult part can be in accepting the changes that meet us along the road. I'm not just talking about religious life. There are relatively few people in religious life, compared with the millions of single and married folk. Nonetheless, anyone who tries to live according to God's will, finds themselves on a great adventure. The more open we are to God, the further He guides us. It's an extraordinary journey, but one which not that many people are really open to. The temptation is to keep things "under control" and only allow what we are comfortable with. But God wants to take us from our comfort zone and this is where we need to trust in His providence—easier said than done!

God grant me the serenity to accept the things I cannot change;

Courage to change the things I can;

And the wisdom to know the difference. (*The Serenity Prayer*)

BACK TO MINISTRY

After I'd been out of ministry for about four months, I began to work in a parish north of Galway, called Oughterard. Oughterard is a picturesque village at the gateway to Connemara, and a popular spot for tourism and fishing. This assignment gave me a chance to gradually and gently return to ministry, as I wasn't under too much pressure. I was amazed at how much my confidence had been shaken after burning out. However, God is kind and understanding, and I worked with a wonderful priest by the name of Patrick Heneghan. The few months I had in Oughterard helped me to get back on my feet, not least thanks to Fr. Patrick's kindness.

That June my bishop told me that in September I would be allowed to continue the other half of my licentiate in theology. During my final year in the seminary I'd completed the first half of this course, which was similar to a two-year master's degree and qualified me to teach theology in a seminary. To my surprise, the bishop added that he'd be open to me continuing studies after the licentiate, if I was interested. I'd not been expecting this, but I was absolutely delighted at the possibility.

As part of the licentiate you're required to write a thesis. I was specializing in mystical theology (also known as spiritual or ascetical theology), but I'd no idea what to write my thesis on. My director came up with various suggestions, but none of them really grabbed me. Finally he said, "What about doing something on St. Thérèse of Lisieux?" This definitely interested me and so I decided to study her life and work.

St. Thérèse of Lisieux was a French Carmelite nun who died on the 30th September 1897, at the age of only twenty-four. I'd read a little about Thérèse and she seemed like a very interesting young woman who'd been given some profound insights into life. Since her death she had been made a doctor of the Church, which means that her ideas and writings had been recognized for their profundity. As I began to read more about her I discovered that she had been through agony before she died—even to the point of wanting to commit suicide because of the pain she was going through. She had also had the experience of "unbelief," where everything she believed in and dedicated her life to seemed to disappear. Dreadful though her suffering was, it had brought about an inner transformation. She had passed through what is sometimes called the "dark night of the soul," a kind of intense purification and inner transformation that God brings about in a soul in order to bring that soul closer to Him. It could be described as a final getting ready to be with God.

I found that I could relate to some of the sufferings Thérèse had been through; having been through an ordeal myself helped me to write about her. It's very encouraging to read about someone else's struggles and see how they came out the far side richer for the torment. If I'd not had to struggle in the way I had, I don't think I'd have been able to relate to her as well. Halfway through my studies of St. Thérèse, I received an opportunity to make a pilgrimage to Lisieux, where Thérèse had spent most of her life. It was wonderful to stand in the house where she grew up, and pray in the convent where she spent the last nine years of her life. When you study anyone in great detail it feels like you're looking at the world through their eyes. To be able to visit the places where she lived made it even more personal.

Many people's impression of Thérèse is simply of a sweet young woman with a very romantic view of religious life, who'll give you flowers as a sign that your prayers to her have been answered. However, I believe it's worth getting to know her in greater depth, as you'll discover a fascinating lady who made every effort to give herself completely to God, and was brought to great holiness in a short time. It was really only thanks to the publication of her autobiography the year after her death that people began to realize what an extraordinary woman she was, as she didn't make a noticeable impression during her life. Like Thérèse, many souls who are close to God often go unnoticed.

Chapter Eight

ALL ROADS LEAD TO ROME

WHEN I FINISHED MY LICENTIATE in theology the bishop told me I could go to Rome for a doctorate. I'd been toying with this idea for the whole year and found it difficult to know whether I should go or not. I wasn't confident that I'd be up for it, but I was encouraged to go and so I decided to take the chance.

In September 2002, I flew to Rome and spent the first few days trying to settle down in the Pontifical Irish College, just off John Lateran Square. I met a man by the name of Michael Courtney—whom I later discovered was an archbishop and the papal nuncio (or pope's representative) in Burundi—a few times over breakfast. He came across as very intelligent, although he didn't say much. I didn't know who he was at the time, as he was very informal and casually dressed. In 2003, he was ambushed in Burundi and shot dead, attempting to negotiate a peace agreement between the Hutus and Tutsis, two warring factions in the country. Apparently, some extremists had decided to kill him, and had sprayed his car with bullets, hitting him three times. It was only after his death that I began to learn what an extraordinary man he was. Looking back, what impressed me most was the fact that he was so unassuming, with no "airs and graces,"—just like so many others who serve God quietly in the Church and generally go unnoticed. He was now yet another martyr.

Shortly after we started the academic year, my fellow students and I were given an official letter of welcome from the rector Monsignor Liam Bergin. Among the various things he said in the letter, he mentioned how post-graduate studies can often be a time of crisis in a person's life. This was the last thing I wanted to hear, as I was just after coming out of a major one! It seemed ironic. I began studying in the University of St. Thomas Aquinas, better known as "the Angelicum." (The name "Angelicum" comes from the name "the angelic doctor," which was a nickname given to St. Thomas Aquinas.)

The three years I spent in the Irish College was one of the best experiences I've ever had of a Christian community. It may sound strange, but religious houses don't always feel like Christian communities! However, this was certainly not the case in Via dei Santi Quattro, the street where the college is located. Because there are no longer enough Irish priests and seminarians to fill the college, it's now very international. There were priests and seminarians from up to twenty-one different countries at the college. Living with people from all over the world was an education in itself— in all senses of the word. When you have someone from Switzerland organizing the serving rota in the refectory, you expect everything to run with precision; except many of those serving were Irish, Italian, and African and had a very different way of thinking from the Swiss! You can imagine the fun. In spite of these cultural issues, we generally got on very well and had a great sense of brotherhood. People looked out for each other and helped each other in many inspiring and generous ways.

One real eye-opener for me was that many of the priests studying with me were very poor. They had to work in parishes at the weekends simply to earn enough to survive. I was looked after by my diocese and was paid regularly, for which I was very grateful. I began to understand that most of the African priests depended completely on their bishops to give them offerings for masses, which the bishops in turn received from the Vatican. Otherwise, they had no income. This is part of the idea of a mass offering, or stipend. When someone asks a priest to "offer mass" for a particular person or intention, they often give a donation as a thank you. This isn't a payment, since you cannot pay for spiritual goods and it would be wrong to do so; rather it's a way of helping the priest survive, and in many countries, these donations are now essential.

Many of the priests from Eastern Europe were in a similar position, although they weren't as badly off as the Africans. One particular friend from Nigeria, Michael Gokum, told me that he'd been asked to start a new parish in Nigeria when he finished at the college. However, he had no church building, no house of his own, no transport, and no money. I was shocked when I became aware of this. We take so much for granted, at least in Ireland. It would never occur to me not to have a house or stipend of some kind, even if not a big one. All of us priests received more or less the same kind of training and were doing similar work, yet the differences in our material circumstances were enormous.

Being with these men also gave me a great sense of what is called the "Universal Church"—that is, the Church throughout the world essentially doing the same work everywhere. Most of this labor is hidden and will always be so; as is the majority of a priest's day. It's spent talking and listening to people about personal matters, visiting the sick, burying the dead, and giving time to prayer, which we believe is one of the most important things we can do. Our job has always been to offer sacrifice for the people and to pray and intercede for them—and through the holy offering of mass we continue to do so.

A MARTYR

For the first year and a half in Rome my next-door neighbor was a young priest from Iraq, called Ragheed Ganni. I wasn't even aware there were Catholics in Iraq until I met him. Ragheed was a very gifted young man—fluent in Aramaic (the language of Jesus), Arabic, Italian, and English, and possibly other languages as well. He knew several phrases in Irish, too, with which he loved to greet the Irish priests. He had a wonderful personality and was very likable. He usually hailed me with "Hey! *Vicino!*" (*neighbor* in Italian) until I moved and then he would call out "Hey! Ex-*Vicino!*"

Having arrived in 1996, Ragheed had completed all his studies for the priesthood in Rome, but had been unable to go back to Iraq. So, after being ordained a priest in 2001, he remained in Rome for further studies. During this time the American invasion of Iraq took place, to overthrow Saddam Hussein. Ragheed was from Mosul in the north—the biblical city of Nineveh. I can only imagine how stressful it must have been for him, knowing that his family and friends were still there and not sure what was going to happen or how safe they'd be. Not surprisingly, he became physically ill during this time because of the stress.

Before the war started I asked him what his fears were for his country. He said that the problem was not the Americans invading, rather when they pulled out again. He indicated that there'd be civil war and that the Christians would be wiped out. Ironically the Catholics (only two to three percent of the population) had experienced complete freedom to practice under Saddam. Once the war started, however, Iraq descended into chaos and the Christians began to be annihilated.

In 2003, Ragheed returned to Iraq—now a very different country to the one he had left. To get into the country, he told me, he had to fly into Syria and then take a bus across the border. I received a few emails from him after he returned. He said that there was a curfew almost every night and it was becoming more and more difficult for the Christian community. One day, he sent me an email with photos of his church on fire. Gunmen had rushed in and had taken him out at gunpoint. He thought he was going to be shot, but instead they blew up the church.

Ragheed was able to return to Rome at least twice over the next three years, and I met him on one of those visits. He'd put on some weight; it was too dangerous to go outside to exercise. More and more among those of his parishioners who could afford to leave had fled, and we worried for his safety. Ragheed knew that staying on in Iraq was becoming increasingly dangerous, but he believed that God was asking him to be in his country. One of the neighboring churches was hit by a car bomb, killing two people and injuring many. The bishop's house was blown up and Ragheed's sister was injured by a grenade thrown at her while she was going to clean the church in preparation for Sunday mass. In spite of death threats and the obvious danger, Ragheed and other priests continued to minister to their people and they in turn continued to come to pray and celebrate mass.

On 3rd June 2007, a friend phoned to tell me the terrible news that Ragheed had been shot dead with three others the day before. He'd just finished celebrating mass and was leaving the church with another sub-deacon, with two other sub-deacons and the wife of one of them in the car behind. A year after the ordeal, the woman and only survivor, Bayan Adam Bella, has had the courage to speak out in an interview she gave to the Arabic-language website for Christians, Ankawa.com (from which the following is excerpted):

"At a certain point the car was stopped by armed men. Fr. Ragheed could have fled but he did not want to, because he knew they were looking for him. They forced us to get out of the car and led me away."

"Then one of the killers screamed at Ragheed, 'I told you to close the church. Why didn't you do it? Why are you still here?'"

"And he simply responded, 'How can I close the house of God?'"

"They immediately pushed him to the ground, and Ragheed had only enough time to gesture to me with his head that I should run away. Then they opened fire and killed all four of them." At this point Bayan fainted.

The killers then left the bodies booby-trapped in the hope of killing others as well. People had to wait five hours for the army to come and defuse the bodies so they could be taken away safely. Not long before this, the three sub-deacons had insisted on accompanying Ragheed everywhere for his own safety, as he'd received several death threats. Their names were Basman Yousef Daud, Wahid Hanna Isho, and Gassan Isam Bidawed. Ragheed was just thirty-five years old and had been a priest for only six years. Here are two moving lines which Ragheed said during his visits to Italy after the war started:

Without Sunday, without the Eucharist, the Christians in Iraq cannot survive. (2006)

Christ challenged evil with his infinite love. He keeps us united and through the Eucharist he gives us life, which the terrorists are trying to take away. (2007)

Bayan now lives in Syria as a refugee with her brother-in-law's family and her own four children. She has been seeking asylum in the West, but so far has met only obstacles.

Three days after Ragheed's death, mass was celebrated in the Irish College in Rome for him. I was fortunate enough to be in Rome at the time and was grateful to be able to attend. A huge crowd attended and the mass was celebrated in the Chaldean rite by Monsignor Philip Najim, Chaldean Procurator to the Holy See and Apostolic Visitor in Europe. Also in attendance were Cardinal Daoud Ignace Moussa; Cardinal Desmond Connell; Cardinal Bernard Law; the Irish, British, and Iraqi ambassadors to the Holy See; representatives of the American Ambassador to the Holy See, as well as many priests and friends. It was also moving to see a young priest friend of Ragheed's called Amer Najman Youkhanna, from the same diocese. In due course, he would also be returning to Iraq.

St. Ignatius, bishop of Antioch before the year 100, wrote seven letters to different communities of Christians while he was on the long journey to Rome to be martyred, because he wouldn't renounce his faith. Astonishingly, Ignatius was afraid that his friends would try to help him escape. "Neither the pleasures of the world nor the kingdoms of this age will be of any use to me," he wrote. "It is better for me to die [in order to unite myself] to Christ Jesus than to reign over the ends of the earth. I seek him who died for us; I desire him who rose for us. My birth is approaching." He pleaded with his friends to allow him to be martyred and not intervene. He saw it as his ultimate witness to his faith. "I am God's wheat," he said. "I must be ground by the teeth of wild beasts that I may end as the pure bread of Christ." His wish was granted and he was killed in the Coliseum in Rome.

Terrible though it is, martyrdom is always of great inspiration to others and an encouragement to persevere. In the second century, Tertullian wrote: "The blood of the martyrs is the seed of Christians." This is still true. My own reaction to Ragheed's death, apart from the shock and the feelings of anger that accompany such an unjust killing, was to make me all the more determined to persevere in my faith. In any way of life, it's easy to become discouraged, and religious life is no exception. An event like Ragheed's martyrdom gives me renewed purpose. It helps affirm my belief that without faith a person's death is the worst disaster imaginable, but if we believe what we claim to believe, then Ragheed is now enjoying eternal happiness with God and is praying for us. The sadness is really for ourselves as we miss the ones we've lost; but we should be happy for the dead, because they're now where we long to go, too. Understandably, people wonder sometimes whether they'd have the courage not to deny their faith in the face of death—surely, the ultimate test for any of us. However, I believe that God gives people the strength to be faithful at that time.

People think of Christian martyrdom as something that only happened in the early Church. However, the twentieth century has had more martyrs than any preceding century. I spent only three years in Rome, and yet I personally met two men who were now martyrs. And it has not stopped.

In March 2008, Ragheed's bishop, Faraj Rahho, was kidnapped and murdered. The Church in Iraq has suffered a great deal.

A FOREIGNER IN A FOREIGN LAND

My time in Rome gave me the opportunity to study many aspects of our faith that I'd wanted to know more about for some time. I ended up doing my doctorate on the writings of the American Trappist monk Thomas Keating, one of the best-known writers on a very ancient form of prayer, which has more recently become known as Centering Prayer. This kind of prayer is something that's been practiced from early Christian times, especially by a group of men and women known as the Desert Fathers and Mothers (or *Abbas* and *Ammas*). They were lay people who began to live in the deserts of Egypt during the third century so they could completely dedicate their lives to God through a life of prayer and simplicity. Most lived as hermits.

More recently, this kind of prayer has been reintroduced to people in more modern packaging, and is helping many people to rediscover the rich tradition of prayer that's been part of the Church for centuries. Many people are under the impression that it's only the Buddhists, Hindus, and other Eastern religions that have any serious kind of mysticism attached to them, and are often unaware of the very rich Christian heritage. Thankfully that is now beginning to be recognized once more.

While I'm very grateful to have been able to spend three years studying in Rome, it wasn't without its difficulties, one of the biggest of which was the loneliness. When people hear that you're studying in Rome, various images of the Vatican, the history, and the wonderful Italian restaurants, etc., come to mind. While I did manage to experience some of that too, the day-to-day reality involved reading books in the basement of the Irish College in a city where I knew very few people and where I was obviously a foreigner. Not being fluent in the language was also quite stressful, at least initially. You took for granted in your own country that when you walked into a shop you could ask for what you needed and be understood. This wasn't necessarily so abroad. You asked for what you needed, but you were often misunderstood and you didn't have enough of the language to explain yourself properly. While I learned a good deal, it was stressful as well.

I've great respect for many of the lay people whom I met studying in Rome. In comparison, it was very easy for us priests and religious, as we came straight to a college or house where we were given accommodation. Everything we needed was provided for, including others who knew how to survive the exasperating Italian system of trying to get your papers in order. Italian bureaucracy would test even the most patient. But many lay people, studying on their own initiative, had to find their own accommodation and work out the system for themselves. They certainly deserve great credit for this.

One lady I became good friends with in Italy was an American religious friend of mine whom I'd met briefly in Ireland. Cynthia was part of a French community called the Fraternity of Mary Immaculate Queen. They're mostly based in France, but have houses in other countries, including one in Ireland, in my home town. I met her briefly in Galway before I set out for Rome and she happened to mention that she was going to be there at the same time, finishing her own doctorate. We politely said that we must meet for a pizza, as you often do in these situations. Not long after I arrived in Rome I tracked her down and asked her if she wanted to meet for a chat. So we did indeed meet for a pizza, just off one of the main squares or *piazzas*, called Piazza Navona.

As we were waiting for the pizza she said to me, "So I hear that you were working in Merlin Park Hospital and that you got burned out and had to leave. Tell me what happened!" I nearly fell off my chair; I wasn't used to people being so direct, especially when I didn't know them very well. However, I told her my story and we discovered that we had a lot in common. From then on, we used to meet almost every week for a pizza and it turned out to be a wonderful friendship. We seemed to be on the same wavelength. Cynthia was a brilliant student. For every book I read, she seemed to read about six. I've never met anyone who could work like her. I've always found that God sends the right people at the right time and Cynthia was a great support to me during that time in Rome. You could say that we were each other's counselors and spiritual directors. She has now returned to teach in the U.S. and we still keep in touch.

One of the joys of living in the Irish College was the friendships that I developed with several other priests. To be studying with other men of roughly the same age, also passionate about their faith, and interested in the same kind of things was a great gift. There were also some fascinating characters at the college, one of whom was John from Serbia. He'd been an army officer in the communist Serbian army—a complete atheist, who'd then had a conversion, become a Catholic, and eventually a priest. He was also an extraordinary computer hacker and guitar player. Sometimes he'd offer to copy programs from the Internet for me, which was illegal. When I expressed my discomfort, he explained that in Serbia you got used to doing things a "different" way, because it was often impossible to do them any other way. Realizing my discomfort he'd then sometimes offer me various CDs or programs and add, with a grin, "They're just *slightly* illegal!"

Another Irish student in the college had worked on Wall Street for a while, followed by four years in the U.S. Marines, before eventually becoming a priest. I attended his ordination in Ireland in 2007. Several of the African priests had witnessed some really horrific scenes in their own countries. One had watched his mother and sister being shot dead before him. The gunman then turned to shoot him too, but the gun jammed and he'd escaped. How one gets on with "normal" living after that, I still don't know. Another student was a Russian named Denis from Siberia, where the temperatures can fall as low as −55°C (−67°F) in the winter. For him to go home meant flying to Moscow and taking a train for one week! Needless to say, he didn't get home very often. I found it consoling that when he stayed with me for a couple of nights in Ireland one January, he said he found it quite cold. The damp air must have made the temperature seem a lot lower!

At the end of the third year in Rome I realized that I would finish the doctorate quicker than I'd previously thought. It had turned out to be more straightforward than expected and I'd also been blessed with an excellent director by the name of Professor Fabio Giardini, an Italian Dominican priest. By May 2005, I was almost finished, but told Professor Giardini that I wanted to wait until the following autumn before completing it. Professor Giardini agreed and told me not to hand in my work too soon, lest I be asked to "defend" it before the summer. (The term used for the final exam in a doctorate is a "defence" or "viva-voce," where the student presents a paper on his work and is then cross-examined by three professors.) As things turned out, even though I handed my work in quite late, the university ended up asking me if I could defend it in June, since one of the other examiners wouldn't be at the college the following semester. This scuttled my plans, but I decided that it would be wiser to go ahead and get it over with. By mid-June I'd defended my doctorate and was finished in Rome. I was relieved. The doctorate was more of a psychological endurance test than anything else, but a great experience all the same. Studying any topic in such detail opens up a whole new world of ideas. I thank God for the opportunity.

Chapter Nine

THE SECOND BUBBLE

THE MIDDLE OF NOWHERE

BEFORE I RETURNED from Rome I telephoned my bishop and told him that I was nearly finished and prepared to take up an appointment in the diocese again. I informed him that I needed a break first, as I was exhausted. The bishop was very welcoming and agreed that a break was in order; however, the bishop—who was about to retire—was suddenly replaced, so nothing was certain. I left Rome and went to Lourdes again to work as a confessor, which I thought would be a break, but in fact was very demanding, and I was really too tired for this kind of work.

While I was in Lourdes, our new bishop called me to say that he was sending me to a remote village called Lisdoonvarna. I wasn't expecting this, as I'd worked there for two months covering for another priest and had found it quite isolating. I'd been hoping for something closer to Galway. However, the bishop asked me to try it at least, and I said I would. Lisdoonvarna is south of Galway Bay, in an area known as the Burren, and a place of extraordinary beauty. People were very welcoming and did all they

could to make me feel at home. I've always been pleas-
antly surprised at how kind people are when I've come to
a new place.

Nevertheless, I found it very difficult to settle down.
I badly needed a break, but with the change of bishops
everything came undone and I ended up without one.
As with Merlin Park Hospital several years before, I was
exhausted but didn't realize it. While I needed a rest, I
also needed the support of friends, but in Lisdoonvarna
I was very far away from anyone. Once again I began to
get depressed and found it hard to cope. On the outside
everyone thought I was doing fine and settling in wonderfully; on the inside, however, I was crumbling. I had
pushed myself hard during my three years of studies in
Rome, and it was only when I stopped that I realized how
exhausted I was. I began to suffer from the same signs of
stress as before, although I didn't recognize them at the
time. I later discovered that it's quite common for this to
happen when someone completes a doctorate, which is
very intense work over a prolonged period. That is why a
proper break is vital. Although it didn't work out that way
for me, it was through no one's fault.

As I started to slip into depression again, a terrible cloud
of disillusionment began to settle over me. This is also a
common symptom of depression. I began to think that I no
longer was able to work as a priest: I was too lonely; it was
too difficult; Lisdoonvarna was too isolating. These were
the thoughts running through my head. I was on a down-
ward spiral. Inside, I felt as though my spirit was dying and
I'd nothing left to give; there was nothing but darkness all
around me. I found myself praying to God to help me, to
show me what I should do; but there was no answer. At my
lowest, I remember standing on the beach in Fanore near

Lisdoonvarna, feeling totally alone and asking God to let me die. It was the first time I remember wishing that God would take me home.

I shared my distress with one or two close friends. Ian—who'd helped me through the crisis when I had to stop working at Merlin Park—was again a great support and source of strength. Knowing me as well as he did, he could see I was sinking. He suggested I go to the bishop. I was reluctant to do this, as I'd only been a few months in Lisdoonvarna. Besides, we were only two priests, with a huge area to cover. However, as I became more depressed and disillusioned I knew that if I didn't do something soon I could end up in hospital. By now I was beginning to feel that I was no longer able to cope with working as a priest. This in itself was very distressing, as the priesthood meant everything to me.

Once again, God began to indicate to me that I needed to do something before I died inside. I eventually came to believe that I needed to stop working as a priest. This was one of the most painful decisions of my life and deeply humiliating. I'd have to tell my family, my bishop, and my friends, as well as having to leave the parish. Nonetheless, my back was up against the wall and I didn't seem to have an option. It was a question of leave, or die. I began to make preparations for leaving the parish, although I didn't tell anyone.

Around this time a good friend of mine, who knew I was in great distress and was praying for me, got a reading from the Bible and phoned me and told me she believed the passage, which was from St. John's Gospel, was meant for me:

When he had said this, Jesus cried in a loud voice, "Lazarus, come out!" The dead man came out, his feet and hands bound with strips of material, and a cloth over his face. Jesus said to them, "Unbind him, let him go free." (John 11:42b–44)

I know that to some people the idea of "getting a word" from the Bible may seem silly, or even childish. However, I've often found that God has spoken to me powerfully through His word and this particular reading was a source of great consolation. In prayer I'd been saying to God, "I'm dead inside, there's nothing left." Here I had a sense that God not only heard my prayer, but was indicating that He'd restore me to life in some way. At the time, I still felt that I'd have to leave the priesthood, at least temporarily, although the very idea of it went against everything inside me.

Finally, I went to the bishop and told him I needed some time out. I tried to explain all that was happening, but I'm not sure if I made a lot of sense to him. I also told my family, which was very difficult, but it had to be done. The diocese arranged a place for me to stay for a few months while I looked for work. Meanwhile, I'd begun to apply for work in different places. The whole event seemed like a bad dream. I didn't want to do this, but I felt I had no choice. I also had to announce in the parish that I would be leaving for some time. Being such a public figure makes this all the more difficult. However, I wanted them to be clear that this was for personal reasons and not because of any scandal.

The day I was to leave the parish was a Sunday. I celebrated the mass as normal in the morning. That afternoon I was also to celebrate mass for a group of children with "special needs." The mass was held in a school hall in the village and many of the children's parents were there. The children would usually spend a little time drawing a picture first and then we'd celebrate the mass together. On this occasion there were three small children about four or five years of age, who weren't special needs, but simply accompanying their parents. Like many children, these three were fascinated with all the things I had in my bag for celebrating the mass. I showed them the lovely gold chalice and dish and the various other things that I'd use.

For the mass itself I used one of the school tables which was very low, as it was for young children. The three little angels who'd been helping me unpack my bag for the mass decided to sit right beside me for the mass. They all sat close together to my left, with their elbows on the table and the back of their palms under their chins. It was one of the sweetest things I've ever seen. During the mass I got one of them to hold the chalice as I poured the wine into it, and another to hold the bowl as I rinsed my fingers. Children love to be involved. I had a great sense of God's love and reassurance through these children. It was as if He was showing me that this was where I belonged, and this was what I was called to do.

After the mass, when I'd finished packing my car, I drove out of Lisdoonvarna for the last time. It was over; I was leaving. How could it have come to this? As I was driving out of the village I had what I can only describe as a moment of grace. All of a sudden the Lord showed me that the priesthood wasn't the problem and that I'd be able to continue working as a priest. In an instant, it became totally clear to me and I knew at the deepest level that all would be fine, even though I had no idea what was going to follow. I was filled with an incredible joy in knowing this and I also understood that God was telling me that I had to go through this whole experience of apparently leaving the priesthood.

It was, I believe, another kind of test of faith. We have our ideas as to what our path is, but if God asks us to do something completely different, are we still prepared to follow? Now, of course, my only problem was how to explain to my family, my bishop, and others, that in fact I wasn't going to be leaving after all! Needless to say, the response I got from my parents and my bishop was puzzlement and concern. They probably thought I'd gone mad, or was at least well on the way. Although I knew that the explanation was going to be difficult, I didn't mind since God had made it so clear to me that the priesthood wasn't the problem. I was in no doubt whatsoever about that.

EASTER

At last I had the break that I really needed, though it certainly didn't come about in the way that I'd have asked for. The whole experience had shaken me greatly. As always, God in His goodness allowed me to get back on my feet gently. I was able to rest and take time to pray. It turned out that one of the priests in a parish not too far away was finding it hard to manage. He was old and quite sick, and I began covering for him, initially for just one or two masses, but then more and more, until I was more or less running the parish. This was another small rural community where the people were very welcoming. They weren't used to having a young priest and I believe they found it very encouraging. I celebrated Easter with them, which was wonderful.

For the Easter Vigil, which is the biggest celebration of the year, we began outside the church in the dark. The Easter fire is ignited and blessed. Then the Paschal candle, representing Christ, is lit from the fire. Everyone carries smaller candles, which in turn are set afire from the Paschal candle, symbolizing the light of faith being passed on to each person. When I came out of the church in the dark to begin the ceremony, I found that everyone already had their candles lit. So, I asked everyone to blow out the candles again, which got a good laugh. One man said, "Father, do you realize how hard it was to light these candles in the wind!" And so we celebrated Easter.

There's always something very beautiful about celebrating Easter with any community. The ceremonies themselves are very moving and full of symbolism: candles, fire, incense, water, oils, darkness, and light. It's a feast for the senses and creates a great sense of the wonder of God's mysteries in our world. Helping people with their faith is an enormous privilege. But I've always found that it's their faith in me as a priest that continues to be one of my most significant sources of strength.

That spring I received a call from a good friend of mine in Perth, Australia. Amanda is a doctor who worked in Galway for a few years and was part of the prayer group I attended. She's a woman of great faith, who looked out for me when I had to stop working in Merlin Park Hospital. I'll never forget her for her kindness. Amanda knew I'd just been through another difficult time and told me that she and her husband wanted me to visit them in Australia. I told her that the offer was very kind, but that it might not be possible financially. She then explained that they wanted to pay for the trip themselves. I was overwhelmed by this generosity but initially felt that it was too much. However, Amanda said that they really felt that God had put it on their hearts to do this, so eventually I accepted the offer. I spent a wonderful three weeks with them and caught up with several other people of faith whom I'd met on a previous trip to Australia. This time away, before my next appointment in the diocese, was a real gift from God, a kind of assurance of how He was looking after me.

By the summer, I felt ready for an appointment. Shortly before the appointments came out (usually at the end of June), I was in a town north of Dublin called Drogheda, where there's a big shrine to St. Oliver Plunkett—another martyr of the Irish Church who'd been killed during a time of great persecution toward the end of the seventeenth century. He had also studied in Rome and was later made archbishop of Armagh (or essentially head of the Church in Ireland). Eventually he was betrayed, accused of treason, and then tortured and killed. On visiting his shrine, I asked him to intercede for me that I would be given a suitable appointment. A few weeks later, I was told that I was being appointed to work in the Church of St. Oliver Plunkett in Galway. St. Oliver had obviously decided to look after me himself.

Chapter Ten

 THE JOURNEY CONTINUES

PROVIDENCE

WHEN I READ the lives of different saints I'm always amazed at what they had to endure and the wonderful, yet very practical ways in which God helped them. The more I continue on my journey as a priest, the more I become aware of the continuing work of God everywhere. Miracles happen all the time, though so often they go unnoticed; even when they are noticed, people can be quick to rationalize them.

A few months ago I was in Poland visiting friends—one of whom was a priest who'd studied with me at the Irish College. He'd since left and was now married, and he and his wife now have a beautiful baby girl. Another friend, Marko, is still a priest and works in Lublin, and I spent a weekend with him. Marko is one of these people with boundless energy who always seems to be doing three jobs at the same time. During the weekend he told me he had to celebrate mass in English for a small group of people, so I went along. There were only about ten people present. Marko asked me to preach in English, so I did.

A young lady called Claire stood up to do the readings and I detected an Australian accent. Afterward, when we were putting the chairs away I asked her if she was from Australia. She said she was from Perth. I told her that I'd been there twice. "Do you know a doctor called Amanda?" she asked. Astonished, I told her that Amanda was a very good friend of mine. She was likewise amazed and told me that, for months, Amanda had been telling her about me and that she should call me. Claire had just started a new community based on the teachings of John Paul II, and she and another friend were spending some time in Poland to learn more about the late pope before going back to Australia to continue their work.

If Claire hadn't got up to do the readings I would probably not have spoken to her afterward, as I wouldn't have heard her accent. The Lord obviously intended us to come together. We met up later that day and she and her colleague told us about the new community they'd started and where they felt God was leading them. Before we parted I said, "Maybe we will cross paths again." She said, "Are you kidding? Of course we will, if the Lord brought us together like this!" No doubt we will meet again. God's providence is astonishing.

I recently became upset about a situation and wanted to go to confession. I decided to cycle into the city to the Franciscan church where confession is available each day from three to four P.M. I arrived just after three o'clock to find notices up everywhere saying there'd be no confessions that day due to construction work going on. I was disappointed, but thanked God for the way He arranges things and decided I'd return the next day. I've learned that it's always good to thank God for everything, even when it doesn't seem agreeable to me. I was probably in the church for less than a minute, but when I turned around to go I noticed that there was a priest sitting just a few seats behind me. I told him that I was also a priest and asked him if he'd mind hearing my confession. He did, and he also told me that he was just passing through on a visit from England. This is another one of the many ways that God reminds me that He's very much involved in the ordinary everyday aspects of my life. It's always reassuring to know that I'm never alone.

PRIESTS LEAVING

At this stage I've come to know quite a few priests who've left the priesthood. For various reasons, they've felt they can no longer continue. I can certainly sympathize with how one can get to this point, having been through it myself. In Ireland at least, the last couple of decades have been a very stressful time for priests—the dreadful scandals have meant that all priests are under suspicion and this caused great suffering for many men and women in religious life who've been faithful to their calling in every way. As a priest you can no longer take it for granted that you'll be welcome anywhere. Sometimes people are delighted to see you, but often they'd be just as happy if you left. I've found that my own generation in particular find it hard to relate to me. As a result they tend not to be too friendly, or will even avoid making eye contact on the street. This can make you feel very isolated. However, I have to remind myself that I'm there because God asked me to follow this way of life. Some will accept me, but many won't.

I remember hearing a story about a young lady who was speaking at a conference for religious leaders during the Second Vatican Council in the 1960s. The different speak-

ers had been talking about the importance of being present to people and making God present in this way. Various
lay people were also asked to address the conference, and
when this woman's turn came she told them she worked in
a big factory in the north of Italy. Most of the people there
were communist, she said. She, however, was a Catholic,
she continued, but she had to remind herself that she was
there primarily for God. If she'd decided to be there for
other people she'd never last; however, if she was there for
Jesus, then she could survive the indifference of the people
around her. Jesus must come first.

This story impressed me, and I believe there's something
very important in what this lady said. If I'm to survive as a
Christian, I must live primarily for Jesus Christ. I'm there
for him and will live in the world as best I can for him. Jesus
can then do what He likes through me with regard to other
people. The best witness that we can give as priests is by
the way we live, rather than by anything we say. As a priest
part of my work is to preach, but unless my way of life is
credible and reflects what I believe, then anything I say will
be a waste of time.

"PRAY, HOPE AND DON'T WORRY"
—PADRE PIO

In my journey of faith so far, God has taught me many
things. One of the most important is that if I'm to survive
as a priest and as a Christian in an increasingly secular
world, then I must be completely focused on and rooted in
God. I must have a relationship with him that's as real as
any relationship with another human being. "Do you have
a personal relationship with Jesus Christ as your personal
Lord and Savior?" is an expression often associated with

Protestant or Evangelical groups, but there's a lot of wisdom in the question. Many people don't believe that you can have a "personal" relationship with Jesus, but you must be able to if Jesus is a real person, and Jesus most certainly is that.

The relationship with Jesus develops over time. For me, it started with those prayer meetings when I was nineteen. I began to discover that a relationship with God was possible and it has been growing ever since. However, like any other relationship it has to be allowed to flourish and will take many different forms. Prayer is the most basic way the relationship is expressed. If you fall in love with someone, you make time for them; if you want to build up this relationship with God, you must also *make* time for prayer, because you almost certainly will not find the time. Even starting with ten minutes each day can make a big difference, because it changes our focus. We realize that we're not alone and that our life isn't just all about us. We're only here on earth for a limited period and, while we are, it is a time for love and service. The sooner we realize this the easier it makes our lives.

Unless we reject that possibility, we're essentially getting ready for the next life, which will be with God. Sadly, many people today live as though this life were everything. If that were true, then why should we think of anyone but ourselves? We might as well squeeze as much out of this life as possible. But if there's a life after this one, which we're heading toward and getting ready for, then that will greatly color how we live. It will also give us strength to put up with hardship and suffering. St. Paul says, "If our hope in Christ has been for this life only, we are of all people the most pitiful" (1 Corinthians 15:19). For any Christian, it's vital that we remember this; otherwise our faith makes no

sense at all. The difference between these two ways of seeing the world comes down to faith. The faith that God has
given me isn't something I can take credit for myself; it is
a gift—the greatest gift that God has blessed me with after
life itself. At the same time, faith is a gift that can be developed, and that is where it is up to us, because God will not
force Himself on us:

> Because of Christ, I have come to consider all the advan-
> tages that I had as disadvantages. Not only that, but I
> believe nothing can happen that will outweigh the supreme
> advantage of knowing Christ Jesus my Lord. For him I have
> accepted the loss of everything, and I look on everything
> as so much rubbish if only I can have Christ and be given a
> place in him. (Philippians 3:7–8)

ᕫᕫ NOTES

1. The Gift of Tongues is mentioned many times in the New Testament: Mark 16:17; Acts 10:44–46; 19:6; 1 Corinthians 12:10, 28, 30; 13:8; 14: 2, 4, 5, 6, 9, 13, 14, 18, 19, 23, 26, 27, 39. It is still experienced by many Christians all over the world today and is acknowledged and approved by the Magisterium, or teaching body of the Catholic Church.

2. The author fully accepts the Church's final decision on the events of Medjugorje.

3. The Poor Clares are an order of enclosed contemplative sisters founded by St. Claire of Assisi in the thirteenth century. They dedicate their whole lives to prayer. See www.poorclares.ie.

4. Taken from the document published by the Yugoslav Episcopal Conference on 10th April 1991.

5. See Laurentin, p. 42.

6. Canon 983 states that: §1 The sacramental seal in inviolable. Accordingly, it is absolutely wrong for a confessor in any way to betray the penitent, for any reason whatsoever, whether by word or in any other fashion. §2 An interpreter, if there is one, is also obliged to observe this secret, as are all others who in any way whatever have come to a knowledge of sins from a confession.

7. This is what is meant by "the Word" in the prologue of John's Gospel. See John chapter 1.

8. It is interesting that most religions have a similar understanding of what we call "Original Sin" or "the Fall," but they give it a different name.

BIBLIOGRAPHY

Buckingham, Jamie. *Power for Living,* Revised Edition (Bristol, England: Arthur S. De Moss Foundation, 1985).

Cantalamessa, Raniero. *The Eucharist: Our Sanctification* (Collegeville, MN: The Liturgical Press, 1993).

Connell, Janice T. *The Visions of the Children* (New York: St. Martin's Press, 1992).

Hahn, Scott. *The Lamb's Supper: The Mass as Heaven on Earth* (London: Darton, Longman and Todd, 2003).

Hinn, Benny. *The Anointing* (Nashville, Tenn.: Thomas Nelson, Inc, 1997).

Keating, Thomas. *Invitation to Love: The Way of Christian Contemplation* (New York: Continuum, 2002).

Laurentin, René. *Medjugorje Testament No. 17* (Toronto: Ave Maria Press, 1998).

Ó Madagáin, Murchadh. *Centering Prayer and the Healing of the Unconscious* (New York: Lantern Books, 2007).

———. *St. Thérèse of Lisieux: Through Love and Suffering* (London: St. Paul's, 2003).

ALSO BY
MURCHADH Ó MADAGÁIN:

Centering Prayer and the Healing of the Unconscious
ISBN: 978–1-59056–107–2

FR. MURCHADH Ó MADAGÁIN unpacks the processes
at work in centering prayer and clears up some of the common
misunderstandings that surround it, while showing
how it is rooted in practices of the Desert Fathers, St. John
of the Cross, and St. Teresa of Avila.

Available at www.lanternbooks.com.